Floridiana

Collecting Florida's Best

Myra Yellin Outwater
and Eric B. Outwater

4880 Lower Valley Road, Atglen, PA 19310 USA

Designed by "Sue"
Type set in Impress BT/Souvenir Lt BT

ISBN: 0-7643-0973-0
Printed in China
1 2 3 4

Published by Schiffer Publishing Ltd.
4880 Lower Valley Road
Atglen, PA 19310
Phone: (610) 593-1777; Fax: (610) 593-2002
E-mail: Schifferbk@aol.com
Please visit our web site catalog at
www.schifferbooks.com

This book may be purchased from the publisher.
Include $3.95 for shipping.
Please try your bookstore first.
We are interested in hearing from authors
with book ideas on related subjects.
You may write for a free catalog.

In Europe, Schiffer books are distributed by
Bushwood Books
6 Marksbury Ave.
Kew Gardens
Surrey TW9 4JF England
Phone: 44 (0)208 392-8585; Fax: 44 (0)208 392-9876
E-mail: Bushwd@aol.com
Free postage in the UK. Europe: air mail at cost.
Try your bookstore first.

Contents

Acknowledgments

Charliene Felts, without whose help this book would have never been written.
Eryc Atwood.
Rasma and Bill Lowry who shared their collections, hospitality, and enthusiasm.
George "Pete" Esthus and his dedication to preserving Sarasota history.
Raymond E. Holland and his invaluable collections.
Carol Front, Curator, Raymond E. Holland Regional and Industrial History Collection.
Doug Luciani of VISIT FLORIDA, an indefatigable resource, always generous, enthusiastic, and helpful.
Cypress Gardens.
St. Augustine Alligator Farm.
Greater Daytona Area Convention and Visitors Bureau.
Greater Fort Lauderdale Convention and Visitors Bureau.
Lee Island Coast Visitor and Convention Bureau.
Stephane Houy-Towner, the Costume Institute of the Metropolitan Museum of Art.
Rick Ferrer, Miami-Dade County, Historical Preservation Division.
Miami's South Beach Marketing Council.
Sarasota Jungle Gardens.
Remko Jansonius, Curator, Sanford L. Ziff Jewish Museum of Florida

About Pricing

Pricing Florida collectibles, ephemera, and souvenirs is more difficult than in most collectible fields since the market place has yet to be defined on a national scale. Most of the objects have been collected for their nostalgic value and were acquired for a few dollars. For the more modern pieces, there has not yet been sufficient time to determine their collectible value since many of these objects are still available on the retail market.

In pricing these items, we have depended on dealers, checked the market place prices and values, and made some calculated estimates. It is still possible to amass a funky, fun collection of Florida collectibles for a few hundred dollars, since many items remain in the $5 to $60 price range. Bear in mind, collectibles of the 1920s and 1930s are already pricey, and more and more collectors are discovering the allure and charm of the fashions and styles of the 1940s and 1950s. Smart dealers are stockpiling items from the 1960s and 1970s. As the baby-boomers age, this generation is becoming more nostalgic for the toys and memories of their youth. Soon, it is likely that the 1960s and 1970s will become another great trove of collectibles.

In conclusion we add another caveat: value is determined only in the market place. When collecting, it is important to find a balance between desirability and economic reality. "Is it worth it?" is a question often asked and the answer is difficult and often a personal one.

As with many one-of-a-kind items, it is the collector who must decide if an item meets his personal collecting needs. We are reminded of one collector whose keen eye ferreted out historical documents worth thousands from a pile of old photographs and papers selling for just a few dollars. And all of us know someone who overpaid for an object just because it piqued his or her fancy, only to realize years later it was a wonderful buy and worth much more than the amount paid for it.

Remember, with Florida collectibles, the key word is geography. A Florida collectible is worth more in Florida than any where else in the country.

Neither the author nor the publisher are responsible for any of the outcomes that may result from using this guide.

Florida, the Sunshine State

"A day without orange juice is like a day without sunshine" says the famous advertisement of the Florida Orange Growers Association. And one of the most amazing sights for the first-time Florida tourist is the sight of orange and grapefruit trees growing in the front yards and back gardens of Florida homes.

Eventually these mansions would become hotels and museums, and twentieth-century tourists and sun-seekers would be dazzled by the range of Florida's architecture from fantasy to elegance to kitsch.

Not only were millionaries and railroad tycoons attracted to Florida, but in the early 1900s, the circus came to town. The Ringling Brothers discovered the Sarasota sun, along with major league baseball (and all the fans that followed). In the 1950s, Hollywood discovered the Florida beaches, and, in the 1960s, Walt Disney sparked a tourist explosion in Orlando. During the 1980s, television writers brought Florida into American living rooms with programs such as *Miami Vice, Silk Stalkings, Flipper,* and the *Golden Girls.*

Today's Florida is bright, colorful, funky, and fun. It continues to lure tourists and visitors south, intrigued by visions of tropical landscapes, poinsettias, lagoons of pink flamingoes, and groves of coconut palms, orange, lemon, lime, and grapefruit trees. Florida has once again been hailed as the fountain of youth by the millions of senior citizens who have settled down there for year-round residence.

FLORIDA has intrigued tourists and visitors for more than 400 years. The first visitors were lured by the promise of gold and perpetual youth. The Florida tourist invasion began in 1513, when the Spanish explorer Juan Ponce de Leon arrived in the New World and staked his claim on the Spanish colony of Florida, a name he chose because it means "full of flowers." Almost immediately, Ponce de Leon announced that he had found his fountain of youth.

In the late 1880s, Florida was rediscovered by a group of millionaire railroad tycoons who saw a treasure chest of gold in Florida's real estate possibilities. These men set up a railway system that connected north and south, which was soon bringing thousands of Americans to the south seeking a winter respite.

Florida became a fabled land of palm tree shaded roadside shacks selling orange juice, quiet beaches with white sand, azure waters, year-round sunshine, and informal living. Millionaires came to Florida and built pleasure palaces modeled after Mediterranean palazzos and European castles.

Florida is a mecca for fishermen and seafood lovers.

The brown pelican is a common Florida bird and can even be found on mailboxes.

Florida attracts birds, beach lovers, and artists.

Gulls, like this laughing gull, are everywhere.

Early risers find the beach filled with tracks as shorebirds scour the sand looking for crabs, clams, and tiny sea life.

Residential streets are lined with palm trees.

But above all, it is the lure of the Florida beaches that attracts the tourist.

Indian Creek is one of the many creeks that meanders through the city of Miami Beach. Scarves and tablecloths with maps of Florida have always been popular souvenirs. This silk scarf is probably from the 1940s. *Charliene Felts collection.* $10-15.

Chapter 1
Traveling to Florida

A 1940s cast iron hitchhiker. In the late 1940s, there was a boom in Florida tourism and everyone headed south. *Charliene Felts collection.* $30-40.

1936 booklet offering a pictorial tour of Florida. *Rasma and Bill Lowry collection.* $10-15.

I first visited Florida as a child in the 1950s. My father and mother packed us all in the family automobile and we headed south. I returned from that first visit with a painted coconut head and a glass flamingo, along with much nostalgia for Florida's white sands, searing tropical sun, clear blue waters, and glasses of fresh pulpy orange juice.

As I grew older, I learned more about Florida. In school I studied about the Spanish explorers and Ponce de Leon's search for the legendary fountain of youth in 1513. I knew of Miami Beach as the place that lured my father and his cronies for "men only" weeks of golf and fishing.

During the 1960s, my parents and I traveled to Florida for a second time. It was spring break, and this time I returned from my Florida visit with a tan and a better game of tennis. I had also fallen in love with Palm Beach and the Palm Beach look.

In the 1960s, Palm Beach still looked Spanish and Mediterranean, and the high rise apartment house extravaganzas of today were not yet on the drawing boards. I was enthralled by the majesty of the stately yellow, pink, and ochre, stucco and red-tiled roofed homes that lined Ocean Drive. You could still see unencumbered views of the beaches and the blue ocean.

My husband shares other memories of Florida: trips with his family where evening wear meant white starched shirts, pastel and floral pants, white dinner jackets, white shoes, bow ties, and summer-weight straw hats. Later, he and his college friends would rally to Florida for spring break hi-jinks.

In the 1900s, Florida tourism would not have existed without the railroads, and in the 1940s and 1950s, without the trains there would have been fewer tourists. The Silver Meteor and the Southern Crescent were among the most popular trains, bringing northerners down the east coast corridor. In the 1970s and 1980s, I could still travel by train, boarding the Amtrak Silver Meteor on the outskirts of Philadelphia. Once on the train, we discarded our winter coats and settled in for a leisurely twenty-six hour trip, arriving in Florida by the next afternoon.

What I remember most from those trips were the glimpses of rural train stops, almost hidden away amidst the orange and grapefruit groves; often only a small, ramshackle sign announced the name of the town we had passed through so quickly and so unceremoniously.

Our arrival in Fort Lauderdale was even more anti-climatic. In fact, without the soft announcement of the trainman, it would have been a non-event. In the first half of the century, train stops such as this were built everywhere by the competing railroad barons, Henry Flagler and Henry Plant. But by the 1980s, Florida's train stations were disappearing, soon to become only pass-throughs off the highways.

With the development of Disney World, in 1971, the Orlando train stop became one of the most popular in Florida, and, with the advent of the Auto-train, many Americans got their first exposure to the thrill of traveling by rail. Not only could they take the train, but now they could take their car with them, to explore the rest of Florida on their own.

The completion of a north-south highway, U.S. Route 1, along the former Old Dixie Highway during the 1930s, also assisted in opening up Florida's frontier to travelers. Soon Americans were driving south, discovering the joy of warm temperatures, sunshine in winter, and all the pleasures of the Florida beaches. In no time, other highways stretched north, south, east, and west across Florida. The Tamiami Trail meandered from Tampa to Miami. Alligator Alley sliced through the state and, in 1938, the Overseas Highway opened, connecting the mainland with the islands of the keys.

Since the 1970s, my husband and I have returned to Florida often. We have golfed at Boca Raton, birded and bicycled in Sanibel, toured Tampa and Sarasota, walked through the sawgrass and the savannas of the Everglades, spent hours on the boardwalks of the Ding Darling and Corkscrew Bird Sanctuaries, and dodged the pot-holes of the Tamiami Trail. We have caught glimpses of alligators, wood storks, limpkins, and spoonbills; paused in gardens filled with orchids, birds of paradise, and hibiscus; tasted coconut milk, mangoes, and key lime pies; basked in the Florida sun; collected Florida shells; bought Florida souvenirs; and marveled at the Miami Beach renaissance.

And, despite having seen and done all that, we're still ready for more!

Maps & travel brochures

Florida maps and historical travel brochures are hard to price. Obviously the older ones will be more valuable than the more recent ones. Generally ephemera can cost $5 to $15 and higher depending on age and value. Scrapbooks are the best source of ephemera and old scrapbooks will bring in anywhere from $15 to upwards of $100 depending on where they are found. Old albums can be found for a few dollars at a lawn sale or flea market. Antiques stores and old print shops will sell the same materials for much more. This is still an uncharted market but one that is attracting more and more attention from collectors.

It is hard to price individual papers or cards. Old brochures can be picked up at a yard sale for as little as 25¢ or for anywhere up to $25 in an antiques shop. Obviously the material in an antiques shop would be more selective since dealers choose material typically for its historical value.

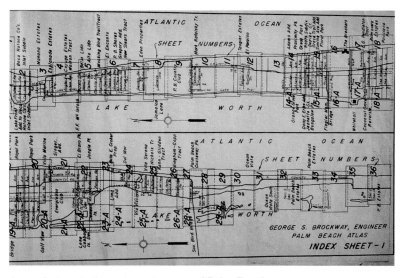

An early twentieth-century city map of Palm Beach.
Raymond E. Holland collection. $5-10.

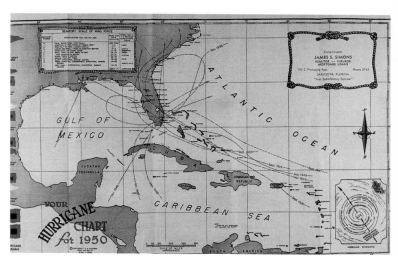

Hurricanes have always been an autumn peril for Florida residents who learn the ups and downs of installing hurricane shutters quickly. *The George "Pete" Esthus collection*. $5-10.

A 1976 Florida Bicentennial map showing 500 years of Florida's history. The Seminole Indians played an important role in Florida's early history. $15-20. (Bicentennial items have value to Bicentennial collectors as well.)

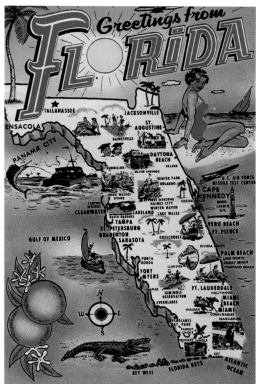

Florida postcards boast of sunshine, bathing beauties, and oranges. After the 1963 assassination of John F. Kennedy, Cape Canaveral was renamed Cape Kennedy. In 1969, Florida residents voted to return to its original name. Today the area is called Cape Canaveral again, but the space center is called the John F. Kennedy Space Center. $1-5.

Late 1940s to early 1950s travel brochure and postcard set. Until the 1960s when Castro overthrew Batista, Havana, Cuba, was a popular tourist destination requiring no passport for Americans. *Rasma and Bill Lowry collection*. $10-15.

Maps of Florida can also be found printed on other Florida collectibles and souvenirs such as tablecloths, scarves, handkerchiefs, plates, trays, ashtrays, and so on. Here are a sampling of items you might find.

A 1960s tin litho plate showing a map of Florida. (Natives call these plates "tacky trays.") The plate can be dated by the name Cape Kennedy. Cape Canaveral was renamed Cape Kennedy after Kennedy's assassination, but, in 1969, the name was changed back to Cape Canaveral. Note the bikini bathing suit, which helps date the plate. *Creative Collections.* $10-15.

Notice that this is a later plate because the Space Center has been renamed Cape Canaveral and Disney World is a large presence. *Creative Collections.* $10-20.

This 1970s plate calls "Disney World," "Disney Land." $15.

This plate can be dated because Epcot was built in the 1980s. $20-25.

Tablecloths and fabrics from the 1940s-1960s are priced in the $35 to $80 range. Value depends on color, design, and condition. Cotton and silk cloths command higher prices than those of polyester or synthetic materials. Florida collectors especially like those fabrics with Florida designs and motifs. Those with maps and tourist attractions are particularly popular and desirable. Tablecloths can be dated by the hairdos, beach fashions, colors (pink and black were typical 1950s colors), and place names that appear on them. For example, Bradenton was usually not listed on its own but grouped under Sarasota until the 1950s; Cape Canaveral became Cape Kennedy briefly in the mid 1960s; and Disney arrived in Orlando after 1970. The west coast of Florida can be dated by the Sunshine Highway Bridge, which crosses Tampa Bay. The first bridge, built in 1954, was a double span. A new single span bridge was built in 1987. Cuban motifs appeared as popular designs pre-1960s.

Cotton tablecloths in the 1940s and 1950s showed maps of Florida, typical Florida scenes, Florida birds, and Florida flowers. This 1950s tablecloth shows one of Tampa's famous landmarks, the Sunshine Highway Bridge, which was built in 1954. In 1980, a freighter hit one of its spans and caused considerable damage. In 1987, a newer, sleeker single-span bridge replaced the earlier bridge. *Rasma and Bill Lowry collection.* $35-60.

A 1950s handkerchief. Hibiscus flowers have always been popular Florida symbols. Although Bradenton was founded in the 1920s, for many years it was grouped under the name of Sarasota. Beginning in the 1950s, the town of Bradenton was listed separately on souvenir maps of the Sarasota area. *Rasma and Bill Lowry collection.* $10-15.

Another 1950s handkerchief. Until the 1980s, most visitors seemed to prefer the more populated east coast to Florida's west coast. Since the 1980s, the west coast has experienced a new influx of tourism. *Rasma and Bill Lowry collection.* $10-15.

This 1950s tablecloth uses three colors—black, pink, and green. *Charliene Felts collection.* $30-50.

A 1950s batiste handkerchief showing flamingoes, fish, and coconut palms. *Charliene Felts collection.* $10-15.

License Plates

License plates sell for anywhere from $5 and up. The general range is $10 to $15. There is big market for reproduction license plates, so if a license plate looks too good to be true, it may be a "repro." Prices for older plates are determined by condition and fading.

A typical 1940s-1950s car plate proclaiming that Sarasota, Florida, was an "air-conditioned city." In the late 1940s and 1950s, hotels used air-conditioning as a big draw for tourists. The advent of air-conditioning was important throughout the south, changing the way of life and many building designs. Before the installation of air-conditioning became common, traditional-style Florida "cracker" houses were designed so that their screened windows would capture the north-south sea breezes. Note the Marlin and the ubiquitous palm tree. *The George "Pete" Esthus collection.* $25-35. (This would be worth more if in better condition.)

An early 1940s car plate boasting that Clearwater was the Springtime city. A typical Florida symbol, the bathing beauty perches on another typical Florida symbol, a palm tree. This kind of decorative car element is valued at $500-600. *Charliene Felts collection.*

14

A 400th anniversary of Florida settlement license plate. The area now known as Florida was the site of the first European colony in America. Ponce de Leon arrived in 1513. *The George "Pete" Esthus collection.* $10.

A 1950s car plate proclaiming Sarasota as Florida's entertainment capitol. Until the explosion of the Walt Disney empire in Orlando, in 1971, Sarasota was the entertainment capital of Florida for most of the twentieth century. In 1927, the city became the winter headquarters of the Ringling Brothers Circus. And, in the 1950s, Sarasota became a magnet for Hollywood producers who began to make circus and beach movies. *The George "Pete" Esthus collection.* $10.

One of many popular circus car plates from the 1950s. *The George "Pete" Esthus collection.* $10-15.

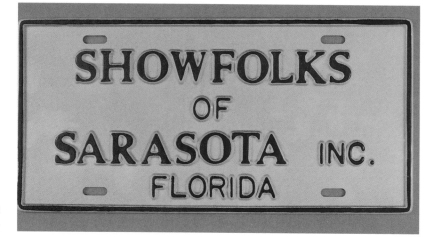

Another car plate. *The George "Pete" Esthus collection.* $10.

This 1980s motorcycle plate has no logo. *Eryc Atwood collection.* $5.

A 1999 Florida license plate showing that Florida is the Sunshine State. Today Florida license plates advertise *every* aspect of Florida life, from the panther, the official state animal, to the manatee, the official state mammal, to the state flower, the orange blossom.

No longer just a vacation place, Florida is building its image as an arts capital and, indeed, within the last twenty years, more and more museums, theaters, and arts centers have sprung up in what were formerly just beach resorts. Cities such as Palm Beach, Sarasota, Daytona, and Boca Raton, as well as Miami, boast a complete year-round performing arts schedule.

Florida oranges.

And, of course, Florida has become one of the center's of the modern space age.

17

The Spanish established what would become the first European settlement in Florida in the colonial city of St. Augustine in 1565.

Early twentieth-century pen and ink sketches of St. Augustine. In a 1887 book, St. Augustine is called the American Riviera, the winter Newport. *Raymond E. Holland collection.* $5 each.

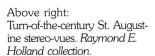

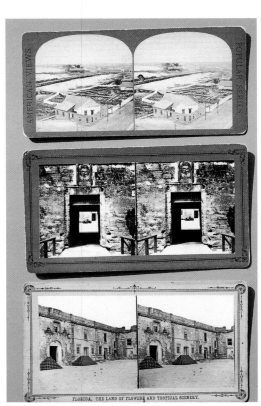

Left:
Charlotte Street—
St. Augustine,
Florida.

Above right:
Turn-of-the-century St. Augustine stereo-vues. *Raymond E. Holland collection.*

Right:
Stereo-vues of St. Augustine and the old Spanish Fort. $5 each.

An early twentieth-century, hand-painted souvenir plate of the Slave Market in St. Augustine. Plates like these can be priced $25-45. *Raymond E. Holland collection.*

Another early twentieth-century souvenir plate of the Old City Gates in St. Augustine. *Raymond E. Holland collection.*

An early twentieth-century Limoges souvenir plate trimmed with gold of the Old City Gates in St. Augustine. *Raymond E. Holland collection.* $50-75.

Five national flags have flown over Florida—the Spanish, the French, the English, the United States, and the Confederate. In 1763, England gained control of the colony of Florida, but ceded it back to Spain in 1783. Florida formally became a part of the United States in 1821, became a state in 1845, seceded from the Union in 1861, and became a state again in 1868, after the Civil War.

A Florida chain gang—not everyone lived so well.

Northern Florida lifestyle, 1880s. Vintage black and white photographs: $2-5.

Today millions of tourists who travel to Florida owe their thanks to two Henrys, Henry Flagler and Henry Plant. Both men realized Florida's tourist potential late in the nineteenth century. Like many of the great capitalist barons of the era, these two men were intrigued with the restorative nature of Florida's climate and the financial possibilities held by its miles of undeveloped beach front.

It was Henry Flagler's vision of an east coast railway that developed the first winter resorts of Palm Beach and Daytona Beach.

Served in Palm Beach, a cookbook compiled by the guild of the Church of Bethesday-by-the-Sea, "with grateful acknowledgment to the winter residents of Palm Beach whose delightful recipes . . . made [the] enterprise possible." $10-15.

The railroads opened up Florida.

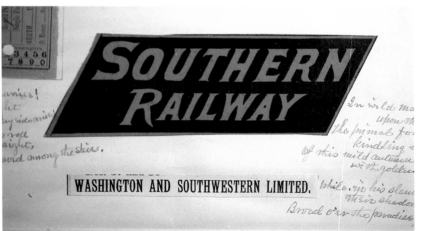

20

No. 3.—In Effect Dec. 23, 1895.

TIME TABLES
OF THE

Florida East Coast Railway.

JOSEPH RICHARDSON,
General Passenger Agent.

SOUVENIR

COTTON STATES
AND
INTERNATIONAL
EXPOSITION
ATLANTA, GA.
U·S·A
SEPT·18·TO·DEC·31
···· 1895 ····

CENTRAL
and
East Coast
OF
FLORIDA

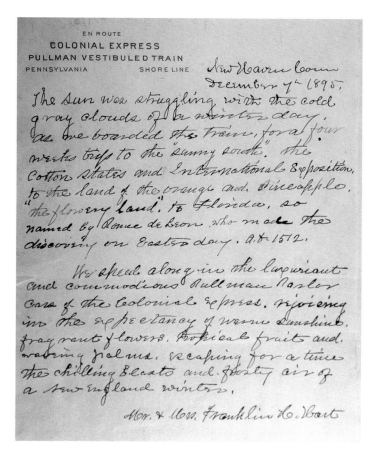

EN ROUTE
COLONIAL EXPRESS
PULLMAN VESTIBULED TRAIN
PENNSYLVANIA   SHORE LINE

New Haven Conn
December 7th 1895.

The sun was struggling with the cold gray clouds of a winter day, as we boarded the train, for a four weeks trip to the "sunny south", the Cotton States and International Exposition, to the land of the orange and Pineapple. "the flowery land", to Florida, so named by Ponce de Leon who made the discovery on Easter day. A.D. 1512.

We speed along in the luxuriant and commodious Pullman Parlor cars of the Colonial Express. rejoicing in the expectancy of warm sunshine, fragrant flowers, tropical fruit and waving palms. escaping for a time the chilling blasts and frosty air of a New England winter.

Mr. & Mrs. Franklin H. Hart

SOUTHERN RAILWAY
AND
FLORIDA CENTRAL
AND
PENINSULAR R·R·

Flagler, who had first visited Florida in 1878, realized that in order to convince people to ride his railroads, he needed to create hotels or pleasure palaces along the way. His first foray in hotel management was the Ponce de Leon Hotel in St. Augustine, which was built in 1895. It was an enormous hotel built in the Spanish Mission style.

Henry Flagler brought Spanish elegance to Florida—The Ponce de Leon Hotel, St. Augustine.

Today, the hotel is Flagler College. Flagler's next hotel was the Hotel Ormond in Daytona. By the 1890s, he had completed another hotel in Palm Beach, the Royal Poinciana Hotel on Lake Worth.

Flagler's Ponce de Leon Hotel is now a small college in St. Augustine where the students are unaware that the stained glass windows in the cafeteria were created for Flagler by Louis Tiffany and are now priceless treasures.

By 1896, Flagler's East Coast Railway system extended as far south as Miami where he built the Royal Palm Palace Hotel. Up until this point, Miami had been a small village at the edge of a swamp. In 1903, he built the Palm Beach Hotel, which was renamed the Breakers because it overlooked the waves of the Atlantic Ocean. Realizing that the railroad was the key to Florida's expansion, Flagler extended the rail line to Key West, and, by 1912, succeeded in connecting Florida to the rest of the nation.

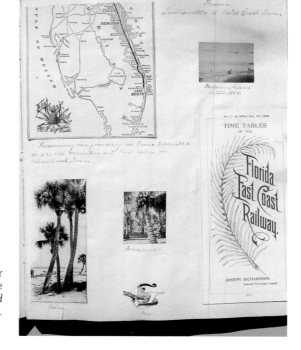

An 1895 railway timetable. This passenger took a trip from Titusville, just north of Cape Canaveral, to the Palm Beach Inn. *Raymond E. Holland collection.* $5-10.

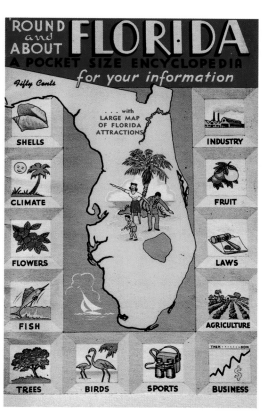

A 1930s Florida tourist booklet. *Charliene Felts collection.* $25.

1895 railway map, photographs, and rail souvenirs. *Raymond E. Holland collection.* $5-15.

1895 photographs and travel brochures showing the St. John's River in Jacksonville. The St. John's, the St. Augustine and Palatka, and the St. John's and Halifax were pre-existing railways before Flagler arrived in Florida. Flagler was the first to connect them and thus offer a direct, uninterrupted service from Jacksonville to Daytona. *Raymond E. Holland collection.* $5-10.

A 1920s-1930s brochure suggesting short motor trips around the Orlando area. *Raymond E. Holland collection.* $10.

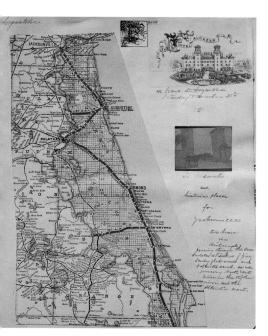

The Hotel Alcazar, another Flagler hotel, in St. Augustine. This railroad map shows the route from Jacksonville to St. Augustine to Ormond. *Raymond E. Holland collection.* $5.

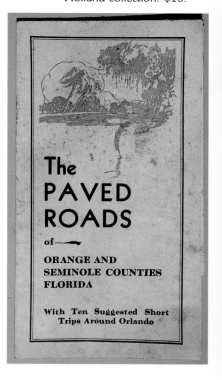

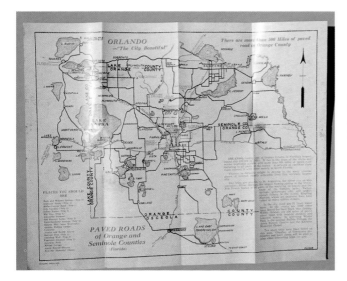

A very early road map. *Raymond E. Holland collection.* $10.

Good Morning

Welcome to our Dining Car

(Please order by letter and list each item desired as waiters are not permitted to serve oral orders.)

A—$1.00

Chilled Fruit Juice
Hot or Dry Cereal with Cream
Hot Rolls, Toast or Southern Corn Muffins
Citrus Marmalade

Coffee   Tea   Milk

B—$1.25

Chilled Fruit Juice
One Egg "Any Style"
Hot Rolls, Toast or Southern Corn Muffins
Citrus Marmalade

Coffee   Tea   Milk

Club Breakfasts

(Please order by number and list each item desired as waiters are not permitted to serve oral orders.)

Choice of Fruits, Juices, or Cereals with Cream

1. Two Eggs "Any Style" $1.35
2. Two Eggs Scrambled with Chopped Ham $1.50
3. One Egg "Any Style" with Bacon or Ham $1.60
4. Brown Corned Beef Hash with Poached Egg $1.60
5. Kippered Herring with Scrambled Eggs $1.65
6. Two Eggs "Any Style" with Bacon, Ham or Country Sausage ... $1.75
7. Griddle Cakes with Country Sausage $1.75
8. Creamed Chipped Beef on Toast $1.75

•

Breakfast Rolls, Toast or Southern Corn Muffins
Citrus Marmalade — Guava Jelly

•

Coffee   Tea   Milk

•

A la Carte Selections Available

Meals on the trains were elaborate, well served, and formal. *The George "Pete" Esthus collection.* $3.

Luncheon Suggestions

(Please order by letter and write on meal check each item desired)

A—$1.65

Steamed Frankfurters with Sauerkraut
Assorted Bread
Florida Orange Pudding with Whipped Cream

Coffee   Tea   Milk

B—$1.85

Tomato Stuffed with Chicken Salad
Saltines
Florida Orange Pudding with Whipped Cream

Coffee   Tea   Milk

C—$2.00

Hot Corned Beef Sandwich on Rye Bread
(Double Deck)
Dill Pickle
Potato Chips
Florida Orange Pudding with Whipped Cream
Coffee   Tea   Milk

Table d'Hote Luncheons

(Please order entree by number and write on meal check each item desired, as waiters are not permitted to accept or serve oral orders.)

Choice
Cold Vichyssoise   Consomme, Hot or Jellied
Chilled Grape Juice

(Price after entree includes the complete meal)

1. Fried Filet of Sole, Tartar Sauce $2.35
2. Golden Omelette with Bacon $2.50

Choice of Two

Lyonnaise Potatoes   Buttered Peas
New Carrots, Vichy

Assorted Bread   Luncheon Rolls

Choice

Ice Cream with Wafers   Plums in Syrup
Chilled Melon   Florida Orange Pudding with Whipped Cream

Coffee   Tea   Milk

Our Special Double Deck Sandwiches and
A la Carte Selections Available

6-1-57

A 1957 Luncheon menu. *The George "Pete" Esthus collection.* $3.

By 1947, there were five Class One railroads entering Florida: the Atlantic Coast Line, the Louisville and Nashville, the Southern, the St. Louis and San Francisco Line, and the Seaboard. The Florida East Coast Railroad continued to provide service within the state. The earliest Florida trains had such romantic names as the Everglade Dixie Flyer, the Floridian, the Silver Meteor, and the Southern Crescent. *The George "Pete" Esthus collection.*

The Mira Mar (beautiful sea) was one of the grandest hotels in Sarasota in the 1920s. In the 1930s, it was bought by the Ringling family and became the John Ringling Towers. *The George "Pete" Esthus collection.* $10.

Dinner Suggestions

Train 6-1-57

(Please order by letter and list each item desired)

A—$1.75

Baked Stuffed Green Pepper
with Tomato Sauce
Tossed Green Salad
Assorted Bread
Creamy Rice Pudding
Coffee   Tea   Milk

B—$2.00

Shrimp Salad Bowl
Garnished with Hard Cooked Egg
and Tomato Wedges
Saltines
Creamy Rice Pudding
Coffee   Tea   Milk

C—$2.25

Creamed Chicken on Hot Corn Bread
Choice of One Vegetable
Creamy Rice Pudding
Coffee   Tea   Milk

Table d'Hote Dinners

(Please order entree by number and write on meal check each item desired, as waiters
are not permitted to accept or serve oral orders)

Choice

Chicken Soup, Southern Style   Consomme, Hot or Jellied
Clam Juice Cocktail   Fruit Cup

(Price after entree includes the complete meal.)

1. Fried Florida Shrimp, Tartar Sauce _____ $2.35
   (Broiled Filet of Fish will be substituted on request)
2. Individual Beef Pie, Seaboard Style _____ $2.50
3. Baked Sugar Cured Ham Natural _____ $2.65
4. Roast Long Island Duckling, Apple Sauce _____ $2.85
5. Cold Sliced Virginia Ham and Turkey with Potato Salad $3.00

Choice of Two

New Potato, Persillade   Fresh Spinach with Chopped Egg
Corn on the cob   Buttered Beets

Assorted Bread   Dinner Rolls

Choice

Ice Cream with Crushed Pineapple   Chilled Melon
Apple Pie with Cheese   Creamy Rice Pudding
Your Favorite Cheese with Saltines

Coffee   Tea   Milk

Our Special Double Deck Sandwiches and
A la Carte Selections Available

6-1-57

Meals could be ordered à la carte or table d'hôte. The old-style Pullman porters were soft-spoken gentlemen. I remember one giving me some marital advice. He told me he had been married 60 years and his secret for happiness was never to go to sleep mad and never to argue in the bedroom. But then he added with a mischievous grin, "we did our hollering outside on the porch, and could my wife holler!" *The George "Pete" Esthus collection.* $3.

In 1902, Flagler built his own Palm Beach palace, Whitehall Hotel, as a wedding gift for his third wife, Mary Lily. In its day, it was described by the contemporary press "as more wonderful than any palace in Europe." Calling it "the Taj Mahal of North America," admirers gaped at its 55 rooms and 60,000 square foot living area.

After the death of Mrs. Flagler, a niece sold it to a hotel investment group. In 1925, a ten-story tower was added and it became the Whitehall Hotel. In 1959, Flagler's grand-daughter, Jean, purchased the property back and turned it into a museum commemorating Flagler's life and accomplishments.

A 1940s postcard of the Whitehall Hotel. Notice its ten story tower addition, which was torn down in 1959 when it became the Flagler Museum. $5.

Whitehall Hotel china. Mayer China , Beaver Falls, PA. Examples of Whitehall china can be found in the Flagler Museum in Palm Beach. *Raymond E. Holland collection.* $75-100.

In 1926, the present Breakers Hotel was built by the heirs of Henry Flagler to replace the original hotel, which had burned down in 1923. Its new architectural style was influenced by the Villa Medici in Rome.

A 1920s illustrated book cover with a view of Palm Beach from Lake Worth. *Raymond E. Holland collection.* $5-10.

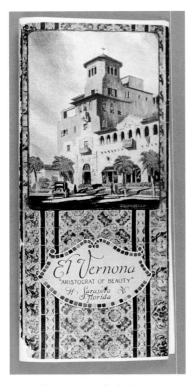

The El Vernona Hotel was called the Aristocrat of Beauty. Built in 1903 in the Mediterranean Revival style, it was bought in the 1930s by John Ringling and renamed the John Ringling Hotel. Today it has been replaced by condominiums. $10.

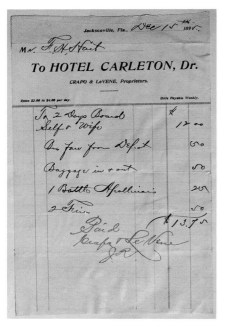

In 1895, rates at the Hotel Carleton in Jacksonville were $2-4 a day. Notice that the hotel charged $.50 to take the baggage in and out and another $.50 for two teas. *Raymond E. Holland collection.* $5.

A typical 1890s FLORIDA CRACKER HOUSE.

A 1920s souvenir plate of the Royal Poinciana Hotel. $50-75.

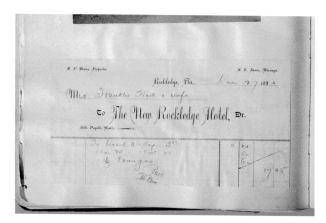

The Harts proceeded down the coast to the New Rockledge Hotel in Rockledge, Florida, where they paid $.60 for a dozen oranges. In 1953, my husband remembers paying $2.00, which he thought was high, for a whole sack of oranges. *Raymond E. Holland collection.*

An early twentieth-century souvenir china cup made in Germany of the Royal Palm Hotel, Miami Beach, another Flagler hotel. *Raymond E. Holland collection.*

An early twentieth-century souvenir plate of the Royal Poinciana Hotel, another Flagler hotel in Palm Beach. *Raymond E. Holland collection.* $50-100.

An early twentieth-century souvenir plate made in Germany and sold by Osky's of the Windsor Hotel in Jacksonville, Florida. *Raymond E. Holland collection.* $35-60.

The Plaza Hotel, Longboat Key. *The George "Pete" Esthus collection.* $10.

February 19, 1906. Fort Pierce pelicans. *Raymond E. Holland collection.*

It was another Henry, Henry Plant, who developed the west coast of Florida by creating a system of railways, paddle steamers, and steamship lines that converged on Tampa, thus creating an important port on Tampa Bay.

By the early 1900s, tourists could travel to Florida by train or luxury steamships. Meanwhile many residents continued to crisscross Florida's interior in canoes and small boats.

Luxury travel. One of the earlier paddle wheel steamers.

Do-it-yourself through the mangroves and Florida swamps.

In 1891, Plant established his own 'pleasure' palace, the Tampa Bay Hotel, at a cost of $2,500,000. The palace was noteworthy for its Moorish revival architecture, its silver minarets, and the fact that its 511 rooms were the first in Florida to be completely wired for electricity. One of the most prominent visitors to the hotel was Teddy Roosevelt who planned his Cuban campaign there. In 1933, the hotel was bought by the city of Tampa and became a museum.

By the 1920s, Florida had attracted a new monied class, the millionaires from the north who came to Florida for the winter and built homes using the castles and palaces of Europe as their architectural models. It wasn't long before every resort had its own group of millionaires. The list of Florida millionaries became a who's who of American industries.

Daytona

Daytona's tourism industry began with Flagler's establishment of the East Coast Railway. By 1889, Flagler's Florida East Coast Railroad had become the principal means of access to Daytona. Like Palm Beach, millionares also settled in Daytona. The area became the winter home of John D. Rockefeller who was called by the locals "neighbor John," and James Gamble of Proctor and Gamble.

In the early 1900s, the automobile was still brand new, and auto drivers discovered that the wide, hard-packed surfaces of the Atlantic beaches were excellent raceways; soon the sport of auto racing was born.

The first auto-race was held in 1902 on Ormond Beach, a few miles north of Daytona. It was a gentleman's race between Ransom Olds, the father of the Oldsmobile, and Alexander Winton, who had nicknamed his car "The Bullet." In 1904, W. K. Vanderbilt set a world's record when his car, a specially-built Mercedes, reached a speed of 92.3 miles per hour.

By 1935, the beach races had ended, but not without the sport gaining international notoriety for the daredevil speeds of the beach racers.

In 1947, a new era of car racing began, when NASCAR, the National Association of Stock Car Racing, was founded. 1959 marked another milestone in race car history, when the first Daytona 500 was held. Today NASCAR and Daytona 500 continue to draw millions of racing fans to the Daytona Beach area.

Auto racing on the Daytona beaches. *Courtesy Daytona Beach Area Convention and Visitors Bureau.*

Early photographs of Daytona Beach. *Raymond E. Holland collection.*

Ray Keech

Photo Album of Auto Racing on Daytona Beach, Florida. Includes photo records of World Speed Record then at 207 MPH in White's Triplex Racer with multiple engines and involving Famous Drivers' Ray Keech, Lee Bible and Wilbor Shaw. There are 20-8X10 and 7-5X7 photos in the album. Photographer: R.H. LeSesne.

Philadelphian Ray Keech was one of Daytona's most famous racers in the 1930s.

Auto racing as a sport continued to spread throughout Florida. An official race report for the 1926 Carl Fisher Cup Race held in Miami. *Raymond E. Holland collection.*

Orlando

Orlando became an attraction long before Disney arrived and created his empire.

In 1895, John Steinmetz, a Florida citrus farmer, converted his orange storage warehouse into a skating rink and built a toboggan slide after the terrible ice storm of 1894 devastated his orange groves. The new toboggan slide attracted local and national visitors.

By 1910, Orlando had a population of 3800. By 1930, this figure had grown to 27,330.

Two photos at right:
A 1950s tourist map promotion for Sarasota.
The George "Pete" Esthus collection.

Sarasota

While Ponce de Leon is the man who discovered the east coast of Florida, it is another illustrious Spaniard, Hernando De Soto, who discovered the west coast when he landed in Tampa Bay in 1539. Sarasota is named after his daughter, Sara de Soto.

In 1925, the Sarasota Chamber of Commerce became one of the first cities to promote tourism. In an unusual step, the city bought a billboard in Chicago and advertised the advantages of coming to Florida, particularly Florida's west coast and Sarasota, in national newspapers.

In 1935, the Sarasota Chamber of Commerce created the Sara de Sota pageant to attract more tourists. The pageant took its name and was based on the story of Sara de Soto, the daughter of Spanish explorer Hernando de Soto, who fell in love with a Seminole Indian chief, Chichi Okohee. Each year local residents acted out their tragic love story and, by 1948, more than 75,000 people were attending the pageant annually.

In the 1940s, a contest sponsored by the Florida Development Board, offering a gold cup to the person who sent the most postcards from Florida, also succeeded in bringing more tourists to Florida. Tourists flocked in by car, train, and trailer. After World War II, many servicemen and their families who had been stationed in Florida during the war decided to settle there permanently. America was becoming a more mobile society and, as a result, more Americans began to uproot their families and seek new frontiers.

A 1920s-1930s tourist promotion brochure. "Spend a summer this winter in Sarasota." *The George "Pete" Esthus collection.* $10.

A 1930s postcard of the Belle Haven Inn, Sarasota. $5.

Before the days of refrigerators, housewives depended on icemen to bring them blocks of ice to keep their food cold. They would hang an ice card like this one on their door or in their window to indicate the weight of ice block they needed. *The George "Pete" Esthus collection.* $25.

A 1950s postcard of the Oyster Bar, a Sarasota hangout. *The George "Pete" Esthus collection.* $5.

A sticker to save the John Ringling Towers development. *The George "Pete" Esthus collection.*

For years the key to the city of Sarasota was given out to the king and queen of the Sara de Sota pageant. *The George "Pete" Esthus collection.* $35-40.

Badge worn by members of the Sarasota High School Sailor Band. The old red-brick Sarasota High School, built in 1913, remained a community landmark for years. When it was torn down in 1958, the Jungle Gardens bought its bricks and created a new red brick wall. *The George "Pete" Esthus collection.* $3.

1948 and 1949 were the last years of the Sara de Sota pageant. *The George "Pete" Esthus collection.* $10-15.

An Indian peace pipe carried in the Sara de Sota pageant. *The George "Pete" Esthus collection.* $35.

A photograph of the newly crowned ermine robed king and queen of the Sara de Sota pageant. *The George "Pete" Esthus collection.* $5.

Miami & South Beach

Miami Beach renaissance—the South Beach experience. In the 1940s and 1950s, South Beach was one of Miami Beach's most popular residential neighborhoods for winter residents. By the 1960s, the area had fallen out of favor, the hotels became dilapidated and rundown, and most of its residents senior citizens. In the 1980s, a group of historical preservationists took a new look at these faded buildings and decided to restore the area's former Art Deco elegance. Today South Beach has become an architectural jewel and a tribute to the Art Deco style.

South Beach was rediscovered in the 1980s and 1990s.

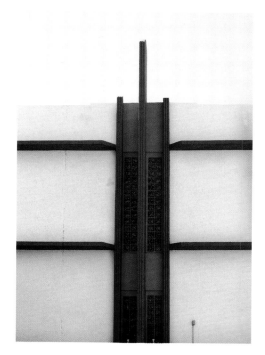

Hotel collectibles

Hotel collectibles are becoming more popular. Their value is determined by whether or not the hotel is still in existence or whether it has been torn down. Collectibles from hotels with historical significance usually have more value. China plates and ashtrays made by Limoges, Staffordshire, or other well-known factories are pricier than unmarked plates. Most hotel plates with historical value are priced at $75 to $100. Others are priced around $25 to $50.

Silver souvenir spoons were popular collectibles in the first half of the twentieth century. Early spoons were made out of silver. More recently souvenir spoons have been made out of silverplate or stainless steel and are mass produced everywhere. Prices range from $2 to $30. Those with historical significance or special interest can be worth upwards of $50 to $100 or more.

La Normandie was commissioned in 1932 by French sculptor Leon Baudry for the French ocean liner *The Normandie*, which was supposed to be a showcase of Art Deco. During World War II, the ship was accidentally set on fire by workmen trying to convert it into a troop ship in the New York harbor. In 1954, the Fontainebleau Hotel bought the statue which is now in the lobby of the hotel's health spa.

A 1930s Palm Beach promotion pamphlet. It wasn't only the millionaires who were drawn to Palm Beach. *Raymond E. Holland collection.* $10-15.

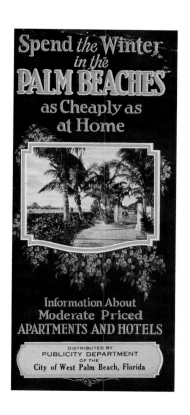

More Palm Beach promotions. This brochure was from 1940s West Palm Beach. *Raymond E. Holland collection.* $5-10.

Detail of *La Normandie*

Detail of La Normandie

Nan Sherwood was a "modern girl who will interest you." A popular 1920s novel set in Palm Beach. *Raymond E. Holland collection.* $15-20.

A silver Palm Beach cigarette case. Smoking became fashionable among women in the 1920s. *Raymond E. Holland collection.* $50-75.

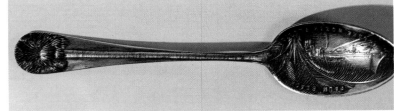

A silver souvenir spoon of Lake Worth and Palm Beach. *Raymond E. Holland collection.* $30-50.

Tiny mustard spoons from Palm Beach. *Raymond E. Holland collection.* $5 each.

More souvenir spoons. *Raymond E. Holland collection.*

A glass tray from St. Petersburg. *Raymond E. Holland collection.* $15-25.

Chapter 3
Tourist Attractions

Sarasota Reptile Farm & Zoo

Snakes have always intrigued tourists. Among the more common snakes living in Florida are the diamond back rattlesnake, the water moccasin, and the coral snake.

More snakes.

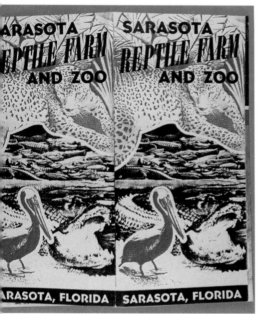

Left:
A 1950s brochure for the Sarasota Reptile Farm and Zoo. *The George "Pete" Esthus collection.* $5-10.

Linger Lodge, on the Manatee River in Bradenton. Originally founded in the 1940s as a fishing camp, today it is an old time trailer park and popular restaurant. Lining its wall are cases of stuffed Florida animals such as these snakes. *Courtesy of Linger Lodge.*

Sarasota Jungle Gardens

In the early twentieth century, many businessmen began to capitalize on Florida's tropical splendor. The thirteen-acre Sarasota Jungle Gardens first opened as a public attraction in 1936. Owner David Lindsay charged 35¢ for adults and 10¢ for children. By the mid 1950s, the attraction spanned acres with tropical gardens that were home to flamingoes, alligators, and even monkeys.

Originally operating as a nursery, the Garden's staff landscaped homes of such wealthy Floridians as John Ringling. By the 1970s, when it was purchased by Chicago White Sox owner Arthur Allyn, the former "impenetrable swampy banana grove" had become a world famous attraction. In 1973, Allyn introduced the first bird shows there and, in 1976, a reptile show was added. Today the gardens have more than 5000 species of rare flowers, plants, and trees.

A 1950s picture guide to Sarasota Jungle Gardens. $25-35.

Canary Island Date Palm

Red Hibiscus and Purple Bougainvillea at the Flamingo Pool

Banana Tree showing Bud and Fruit in Florida

Jungle Gardens Lake Scene

Black Australian Swans

38

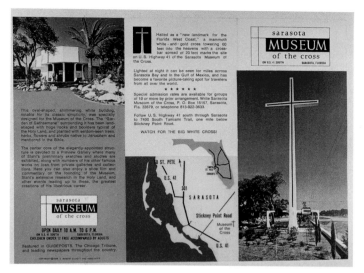

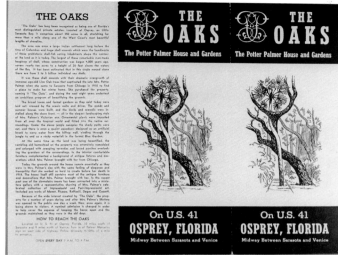

Cypress Gardens

Cypress Gardens was developed by the Pope family near Winter Haven. In 1931, Dick Pope bought 37 acres on Lake Eloise and convinced local authorities to clean up the neighboring canals leading into the property. His dream was to transform this favorite spot of his into "a place where people from everywhere would come to see exotic flora and leave punch-drunk on floral beauty."

When the canal commission reneged on their obligations, Pope and his wife, Julie, worked alongside $1-a-day laborers to finish their "swamp to garden" metamorphosis. On 1936, Cypress Gardens officially opened to the public, offering a romantic gazebo, shimmering bougainvilleas, and Southern Belles. The former "Swami of the Swamp" and "the Barnum of Botany" soon became known as Mr. Florida. In 1943, Julie Pope staged an impromptu water ski show there and soon Cypress Gardens was dubbed the water ski capital of the world. In 1948, Cypress Garden water skiers executed the first two-tier human pyramid, and, in 1953, while filming the movie *Easy To Love*, they executed a three-tier human pyramid. By 1989, Cypress Garden water skiers were proudly showing off three side-by-side, four-tier human pyramids. As a side note, during the 1950s, cypress tree "knees," the gnarled roots of the tree, were highly collectible and were sold as table lamps, tables, and "sculptures." It was very popular to pose against a Cypress knee and there was a widespread curiosity about these trees and their swampy origins.

A 1950s tourist brochure from Cypress Gardens. $5-10.

A two-tier human pyramid.
Courtesy Cypress Gardens.

39

Three side-by-side, two-tier human pyramids. *Courtesy Cypress Gardens.*

A 1950s souvenir plate showing the human pyramid, Esther Williams Swimming Pool, and a human kite. *Rasma and Bill Lowry collection.* $40-60.

A pine needle woven tray of the Cypress Gardens water skiers. Pine needle art is priced and valued according to the condition of the pine needles. Objects should have crisp pine needles, otherwise the raffia connections will fray and come apart. $35.

Weeki Wachee Springs

Since Weeki Wachee Springs was founded in 1946, its bevy of mermaids has become world famous. Synchronized swimming was introduced in 1933 at the Century of Progress Exposition in Chicago. In 1946, a former navy frog man conceived of the idea of breathing under water through an air hose supplied by an air compressor. Immediately he realized the potential for synchronized, underwater dances and the Weeki Wachee mermaids were born. Since then, underwater performances by the mermaids continue to go on for thousands of visitors each year.

We're not like other women
We don't have to clean an oven
And we never will grow old
We've got the world by the tail!
[Weeki Wachee mermaid anthem, 1946-present]

In pricing mermaid collectibles, like other collectibles, their value is determined by age, composition, and personality of the figure. Ceramic and chalkware mermaids can be dated by their country of origin. In the 1950s, most were made in Japan. Today many are made in Hong Kong and China. Generally most mermaid items are priced between $20 to upwards of $100. Pairs are more desirable than singles. Sets of three are more valuable than sets of two. Mermaids made in Occupied Japan are more valuable than those made more recently. Poses are also part of the pricing determination. Depiction of nudity, particularly the realism of breasts, also effects pricing. Since most collectors are women, items with more generalized nudity are preferred rather than figures with extensive or graphic anatomic detail. Mermaid pairs are priced between $20 to $25. Chalkware mermaids are valued at $45 to $55. Sparkle-eyes and pearlized mermaids are also popular. 1940s-1950s Weeki Wachee mermaid sets are very desirable.

This is a 1960s postcard of Weeki Wachee Mermaids. The hairdos are 1960s. $1-3.

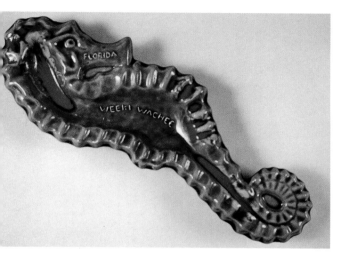

A 1950s Weeki Wachee redware seahorse ashtray. *Rasma and Bill Lowry collection.* $20-30.

A 1950s postcard. Boat neck sweaters were popular in the 1950s and 1960s. Note the shorter hairdos which were popular in the 1950s. $1-3.

A 1960s Weeki Wachee mug. Souvenirs such as these are priced at $25-40. *Rasma and Bill Lowry collection.*

An early postcard showing a mermaid, complete with tail. $5-8.

A Weeki Wachee snow dome. $10-15.

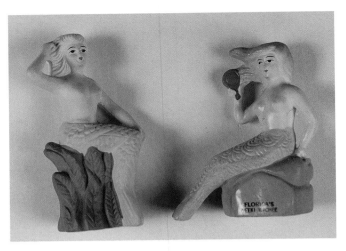

1950s-1960s Weeki Wachee mermaids. *Rasma and Bill Lowry collection.* $10-15 a pair.

1950s chalkware mermaid made in Japan. *Rasma and Bill Lowry collection.* $35-50.

1950s set of sparkle-eyed mermaids. *Rasma and Bill Lowry collection.* $40-50.

1950s mermaid set. *Rasma and Bill Lowry collection.* $35-50.

This 1950s-1960s mermaid shows a gold leaf trim. It is part of a pair. The mate shows an opposing view. *Rasma and Bill Lowry collection.* $35-50.

1960s pearlized mermaids. These can be dated by their flip hairdos. *Rasma and Bill Lowry collection.* $35-50.

1950s-1960s Sparkleware mermaids. *Rasma and Bill Lowry collection.* $35-50.

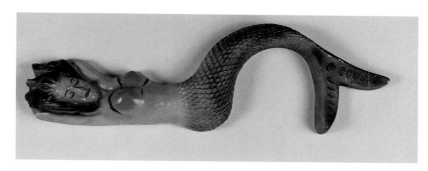

A 1940s chalkware mermaid. *Rasma and Bill Lowry collection.* $45-60.

1950s mermaid. This rear view of a mermaid is unusual. It can be viewed either as a "shy" mermaid or a "naughty" mermaid. The pony tail is very 1950s. *Rasma and Bill Lowry collection.* $30-45.

Chapter 4
Florida Beaches

Florida is best known for its beaches, sand, waves, and surf.

An early morning Florida beach is quiet, serene, and deserted.

Only the birds are at work finding food.

Tables and chairs in the sun.

A 1950s coconut rum candy tin. This can be dated because the pink lettering is typically 1950s. $10-15.

A typical Florida beach scene.

Another tropical beach scene on a 1950s candy tin. $10-15.

An end of the day beach scene.

Alligators

Natural history has always intrigued the upper classes of American and European society, and it has been their money and interest that has been responsible for founding the most famous museums of art and natural history. St. Augustine's Alligator Farm, which is Florida's oldest tourist attraction, was founded in 1893 as a museum of marine curiosities to attract the new group of rail travelers arriving in the town. Soon it became apparent that nothing attracted more visitors and was more curious than the Florida alligator.

With the advent of motor travel, more and more Americans took an interest in the beauty of nature. Florida wildlife could be easily seen, easily discovered, and was exotic enough to want to describe to the folks back home. Baby alligators, alive and stuffed, became popular souvenirs of the 1940s and 1960s and many visitors to Florida took them home.

Alligator souvenirs range from $10 and up. Stuffed baby alligators are worth between $15 to $30. Alligator souvenir bowls, ashtrays, ceramics, and plastic models value from $10 to $50. Mint condition rubber toys are valued in the $75 range. Any toy still in its original box or wrapping increases in value.

Courtesy of the St. Augustine Alligator Farm

46

An alligator on the Tamiami Trail.

Riding an alligator 1900 style. Posing on an alligator became a popular tourist attraction in the early 1900s. *Courtesy of the Sanford L. Ziff Jewish Museum.*

Eat more alligator! Alligator meat has become a popular delicacy. *Courtesy of the Oyster House, Everglades City.*

A 1950s jadeite ashtray trimmed with crushed shells on one side and an alligator on top. Crushed shells were popular in the 1950s. *Rasma and Bill Lowry collection.* $40-60.

An articulated cast iron nutcracker. This is probably pre-1940s since they stopped making cast iron toys during the war. This nutcracker is 12 inches long, is highly collectible, and is worth between $100-150. *Rasma and Bill Lowry collection.*

Another 1950s alligator ashtray. A stuffed baby alligator circles a real shell. In the 1950s, baby alligators were made into children's purses. By the end of the 1950s, this practice was outlawed in a move that predated the environmental protection movement that began in the 1970s. *Charliene Felts collection.* $60-80.

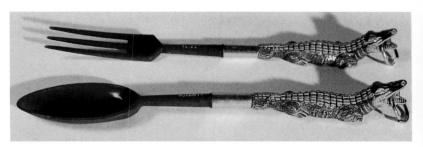

Plastic laminated wood alligator salad servers. *Rasma and Bill Lowry collection.* $10.

Baby alligators, alive and stuffed became popular souvenirs of the 1940s and 1960s. A contemporary alligator head souvenir. Heads like this sell from $25 and up, depending on size and condition. (When standing up or dressed: $75-100.) *Eryc Atwood collection.*

A 1920 silver Palm Beach souvenir spoon with an alligator on its handle. *Raymond E. Holland collection.* $20-30.

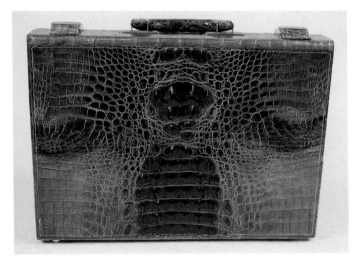

A 1950s rubber alligator toy. Since it comes with its original box, it is more valuable. This toy is valued at about $75. The box increases its value. *Rasma and Bill Lowry collection.*

This alligator skin briefcase sold for $2500. This is a horned back pattern and comes from the back of the alligator. The usual big squares comes from the bellies. *Eryc Atwood collection.*

Two ceramic alligators on a croton leaf. Raising croton plants has become a popular industry. Charliene Felts remembers that her father raised hybrid crotons as a hobby in the 1950s and 1960s. At one point he had more than 3000 plants growing in his garden. Each year he would make cuttings and root them inside. Crotons are valued according to the brightness of their colors. *Rasma and Bill Lowry collection.*

Flamingoes

Although flamingoes are not native to Florida, they have been associated with Florida since they were first imported there from Cuba and Central America in the 1930s. One of the first tourist attractions to capitalize on the exotic charms of flamingoes was Hialeah racetrack. The track, which had been founded in the 1920s as a dog track, became a horse racing track in the 1930s. The first flock of flamingoes imported from Cuba flew away, but the second group stayed and bred, and soon Hialeah's flamingoes became world famous. Today, flamingo items have become some of the most popular Florida collectibles and souvenirs.

Prices of flamingo souvenirs vary from a few dollars to hundreds of dollars. Value is determined by age, color, glaze, pose, artist, origin, and detail of the item. Pairs are more desirable than singles. Upright wings and stretched back poses are more valuable because they are more easily broken and thus fewer have survived intact. Japanese-made or unmarked flamingoes have less value than those marked by artists such as Will George or Brad Keeler. Signed Will George or Brad Keeler flamingoes are worth $250 and upwards. Airbrushing and fine details increase value.

Another 1950s flamingo duo with a hand made ceramic pond. *Charliene Felts collection.* $100-250.

Artists, potters, and designers have been intrigued by the flamingo's graceful, elongated neck and slender legs. The pink feathers also inspire artistic whimsy. It was typical in the 1940s to show flamingoes in a pond. Pairs of flamingoes nesting in a pond remained popular collectibles through the 1950s. Flamingoes can be dated by color and glaze. *Rasma and Bill Lowry collection.* $50-75 a pair.

These Will George flamingoes are not part of a matching pair. They are of exceptionally fine quality with beautiful air brushing. Note the variety of their poses. They are valued in the $250 plus range. *Charliene Felts collection.*

Two 1940s-1950s flamingoes. Will George and Brad Keeler were among a very few artists to sign their work. George's dates are 1930s-1950s. A signed piece has more value and is priced at $250 and up, depending on color, pose, and condition. *Charliene Felts collection.*

Three more graceful flamingoes. The middle one is exceptional for its size and color. The one to the left is by Will George and more detailed and desirable. *Charliene Felts collection.* Left: $250; middle & right: $75-100.

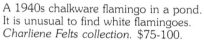

A 1940s chalkware flamingo in a pond. It is unusual to find white flamingoes. *Charliene Felts collection.* $75-100.

A 1950s Will George flamingo with fine airbrushing. *Charliene Felts collection.* $225.

This 1950s flamingo is signed by Will George and shows his fine airbrushing on the black trim on the wings. *Charliene Felts collection.* $225-250.

Note the position of the wings. This is a nice example of fine airbrushing on the foliage. Intricate leaves make an interesting contrast to the graceful pose of a flamingo. These flamingoes are of excellent quality and are in the $200 plus. *Charliene Felts collection.*

"Sarasoda" lemon soda with its marching flamingo logos. *Charliene Felts collection.*

An Italian artist-made 1990s flamingo. *Charliene Felts collection.* $50.

A 2-inch-high miniature woven-grass flamingo with wired frame legs. *Charliene Felts collection.* $45-50.

An early 1950s hand-painted plastic glass with two ceramic iced tea mugs. *Charliene Felts collection.* $25-35.

A 1940s made-in-Occupied Japan ceramic planter. *Charliene Felts collection.* $75.

A 1950s transfer-decal tin flamingo tray. *Rasma and Bill Lowry collection.* $35.

A hand-painted 1950s metal pink flamingo compact. *Charliene Felts collection.* $35-50.

A 1970s wood-like composition plate with hand air-brushed palm trees. *Rasma and Bill Lowry collection.* $25-30.

A hand-painted container. *Charliene Felts collection.* $35-45.

A 1930s-1940s artist-made, plaster-applied-to-wood wall plaque. *Rasma and Bill Lowry collection.*

Flamingo sun lotion. *Charliene Felts collection.* $25-30.

Two 1950s spoon rests. *Rasma and Bill Lowry collection.* $10-15 a set.

1950s wallpaper trim with red stenciling in its original box. *Charliene Felts collection.* $25.

Flamingoes on a 1980s tee-shirt made with rubber squirt paint.

A Staffordshire plate from the 1920s-1930s. This is an unusual commemorative plate. "A Bridegroom, all out-dressed in Red/His bride, who hides her blushing head." *Charliene Felts collection.* $500-600.

A 1940s flamingo design rests on a hooked pillow. *Charliene Felts collection.* $35.

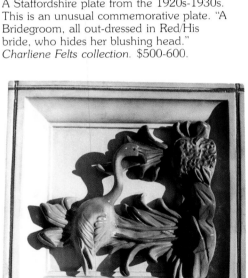

A 1940s three-dimensional chalkware wall plaque. *Rasma and Bill Lowry collection.*

A one-of-a-kind, three-dimensional wall sculpture from the 1940s. Made out of carved coconut shells, it is unusual for a sculpture like this to be intact. It shows a typical scene of pink flamingoes, palm trees, and an orange tree. *Julie Bechko collection.*

Far left:
A fruit label with a flamingo design. Date unknown. *Rasma and Bill Lowry collection.* $5.

Left:
1950s Occupied Japan wall pocket and vase. *Charliene Felts collection.* $20-35.

A 10-inch 1950s ceramic vase. *Charliene Felts collection.* $50.

Italian 1990s vases. *Charliene Felts collection.* $50-75 each.

Two 1930s milk glass vases with flamingo motif. It is known that there is also a green version of this vase, but so far it has not been seen. *Charliene Felts collection.* $50-75.

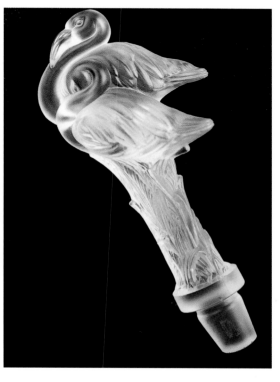

A crystal bottle stopper. *Charliene Felts collection.* $100.

A 1990s oil-on-board painting.
Charliene Felts collection. $30.

Cloth batik. *Charliene Felts collection.*

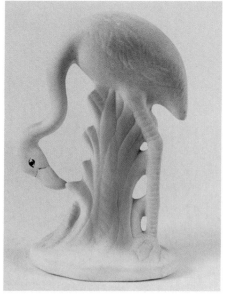

A white flamingo ceramic
mold used in craft classes.
Lowry collection. $10-15.

Left and above:
Eryc Atwood's pond. 1930s concrete
flamingoes valued at $150 a pair.

Plastic flamingo on a spider plant. *Lowry garden.* $20.

A 1930 concrete flamingo in the midst of some 1940s and 1950s concrete and chalkware flamingoes. The 1930s painted metal flamingo is valued at $200 plus. Others are in the $150 range.

Painted plastic marbleized 1940s compact. *Charliene Felts collection.* $25-35.

Man and his flamingo.

Metal Christmas ornament. $5.

22-inch high ceramic statue.

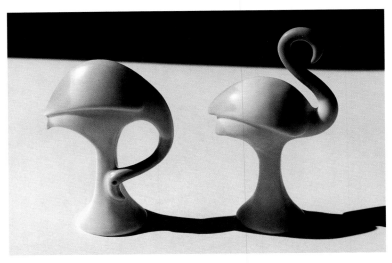

Modern 1980s white ceramic flamingoes.
Charliene Felts collection. $60 each.

Extruded plastic souvenir with artist-made
wooden toy. *Charliene Felts collection.* $10-25.

This flamingo flower frog used as a center-
piece has 1950s air-brushing. $50-75.

Shells

Shell art varies in value. The Victorians loved to create intricate shell compositions. Shell designs were also popular in the 1920s through 1940s. Beginning in the 1950s shells imbedded in Lucite became very popular. Today shells are used imaginatively and are still popular souvenirs. Older historical pieces range in price from $35 to $100. Popular souvenirs of the 1930s through the 1950s range in price from $10 to $50. There is no price guide for shell art made from 1960 to the present.

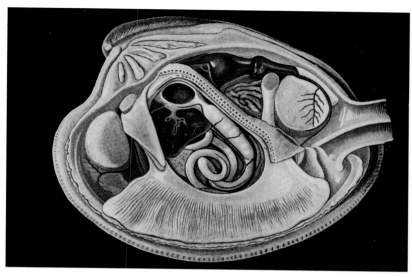

A 1950s postcard of the anatomy of a clam. $1.

Florida beaches are treasure troves for shell collectors who prize the many varieties of shells lying in the sand such as this sand dollar.

A Florida postcard. $1.

Right:
A postcard recalling the legend that the five holes in a sand dollar refer to Jesus' crucifixion. $1.

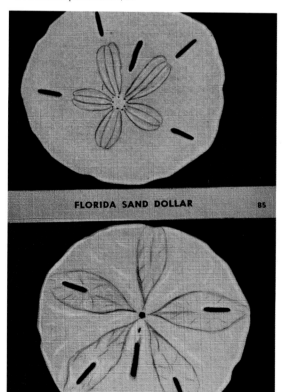
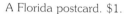

FLORIDA SAND DOLLAR   85

A hand-painted sand dollar. $10.

A shell strewn beach.

The beaches are filled with raw material for the shell artist.

Shells for sale.

1930s shell art pictures with woven pine needle frames. The pine needles come from Norfolk pines or the Florida slash pine. *Rasma and Bill Lowry collection.* $50-75.

Shell boxes.

Another version of pine needle shell art. *Rasma and Bill Lowry collection.* $50-75.

More pine needle-shell art. *Rasma and Bill Lowry collection.* $50-75.

Outdoor shell art.

A periwinkle whelk.

Above and right:
Miss Sea Shell. An original costume sewn by hand in 1918. The dress was made by Fannie Moss of Jacksonville and her mother. Fannie wore it at the 1918 YMHA Purim masquerade ball in Jacksonville. *Courtesy of Sanford L. Ziff Jewish Museum of Florida.*

A do-it-yourself shell cigar box. *Charliene Felts collection.*

Shells on a shell.

A 1930s-1950 Daytona Beach shell souvenir.
Rasma and Bill Lowry collection. $35-50.

1950s crushed shell ashtray and
vase with shell flowers. $15-30.

Lucite and shell bookends. $40-60.

Shell shops held craft classes and taught how to make things from shells such as these shell flowers. *Rasma and Bill Lowry collection.* $10-15.

1950s crushed shell picture frames. *Rasma and Bill Lowry collection.* $20-30 each.

A crushed shell jadeite ashtray with alligator. *Rasma and Bill Lowry collection.* $50.

A ceramic seahorse.

Seahorse wall plaques. $65 a set.

A poured acrylic seahorse. This was another home craft popular in the 1960s. $20-30.

Pine needle art

Pine needle art is hard to price. Most of it falls in the $20 to $75 price range. Value depends on intricacy and delicate handwork.

Pine needle objects became a form of folk art in the 1940s and 1950s. Artisans used the needles from the Norfolk pine to weave baskets, picture frames, and other souvenir items.

A woven Seminole jacket wall hanging made out of palmetto leaves. *Charliene Felts collection.* $25-50.

A 1940s woven pine needle basket. *Charliene Felts collection.* $30-40.

A 1950s woven pine needle tray. Pine needles are easier to work with after they are dried. *Charliene Felts collection.* $35-50.

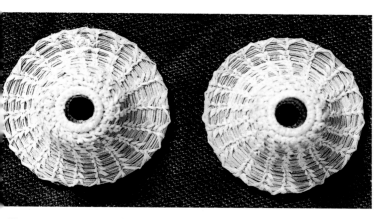

Two woven pine needle candle holders. *Charliene Felts collection.* $10-15.

A circa 1950s woven souvenir tray from Bradenton, Florida. $35-50.

Birds & water fowl

Florida has become a bird lover's paradise. Early morning beach walkers can find willets, sanderlings, sandpipers, caspian and royal terns, ruddy turnstones, gulls, brown pelicans, and blue herons in a span of a few minutes. Visitors to the Everglades can find wood storks, roseate spoonbills, snail kites, anis, purple gallinules, ospreys, and various woodpeckers almost as easily. In fact, for many bird watchers, Florida is a mecca and can yield hundreds of new birdsightings in just days.

Roseate spoonbills at the Ding Darling National Wildlife Refuge. *Courtesy of the Lee Island Coast.*

A postcard from Parrot Jungle. *Rasma and Bill Lowry collection.* $1.

At least five kinds of gulls can be found on Florida beaches.

A 1940s charming little pelican whose bill "can hold more than his belly can." *Rasma and Bill Lowry collection.* $25-35.

A souvenir plate from Busch Gardens. *Rasma and Bill Lowry collection.* $15-20.

A Florida souvenir plate. *Rasma and Bill Lowry collection.* $25-40.

Brown pelicans are a common site on the Florida coast line.

A 1950s "birdy" ashtray. *Rasma and Bill Lowry collection.* $10-15.

A blue heron stalks his prey.

A flock of terns search the beach for food.

A royal tern has caught a bit of breakfast.

Willets and sandpipers prowl the beaches for food.

Coconuts

Coconut heads, while fun to collect, have little marketable value. Most can be bought at a flea market for anywhere from $2 to $20. Older, more intricately carved ones can sometimes command higher prices. Folk art pieces have more value, but we didn't find any of these for sale, so we couldn't assume a present-day value. The only old coconuts we did find were part of personal collections and had been saved by family members as souvenirs from years passed. Eventually they will assume some value in the market place. Beware of confusing an old coconut head for the many new ones made in the Philippines; these are lighter in weight than the old, heavier ones from the 1940s and 1950s.

Above:
Modern coconut monkeys. $10-15.

Left:
A 1950s painted coconut head. Linger Lodge. $30-35.

Below left:
Another funny critter. Linger Lodge. $30-35.

Right:
A coconut dancing girl. *Rasma and Bill Lowry collection.* $30-40.

Tennis playing coconut monkey. $10-15.

Right:
Sea grapes are a common seaside plant.

Below:
Hybrid crotons bear almost no resemblance to their ancestors. Modern growers have magnificently created colored leaves that ring true to the plant's old Indian name "canned sunshine."

Far below:
Poinsettias grow naturally in Florida gardens. Although the red varieties are the best known, the flower also comes in pinks, whites, and with variegated leaves.

Flowers

Florida is one of the few places in the United States where plants and flowers such as hibiscus, crotons, poinsettia, bougainvillea, philodendron, and birds of paradise can be grown outdoors all year round.

Because many of these flowers come from tropical islands, there is a lot of folk lore associated with the flowers and their names. For instance, the name Philodendron means "to love a tree," but during the colonial period, it was called "dumb cane," because the plant's juice was used on slaves who were forced to drink it as a punishment. The juice caused swelling to the larynx and temporary voice loss.

Azaleas are popular in all the southern states including Florida, but few realize that they are native to Java and were first cultivated domestically in Japan.

In the fall and winter Florida's gardens are filled with pampas grass, a grass native to Argentina. Today, these grasses grow profusely in Florida's gardens and in the fall produce sprays of fluffy white plumes.

Because croton leaves come in a variety of yellows, greens, reds, and browns, these plants have been called "canned sunshine." However, today these plants bear little resemblance to their ancestors, because hybridization has produced in them such flashy colored leaves.

The Chenille plant.

The lipstick or firecracker flower.

71

It is hard to believe that the bird of paradise is a member of the banana family.

Center right:
1950s Florida fashion fabric. *Rasma and Bill Lowry collection.* $25-30.

Right:
A 1950s tea towel. *Rasma and Bill Lowry collection.* $10-15.

Colorful croton leaves inspired many fashion designers. These yellow, red, green, and brown leaves, called by some "canned sunshine," have become flashier and more variegated than they were years ago.

1940s wooden photograph cover. *Charliene Felts collection.* $125.

Charliene Felts collection.

1890s photograph of a Florida landscape.
Raymond E. Holland collection. $3-5.

This 1930s Lone Palm Guava Jelly can was made only by the owner's family business in Palmasola, near Bradenton. (Vintage Florida collectibles that pertain to a localized area command higher prices than generic Florida items.) *Charliene Felts collection.* $100.

1890s Daytona street scene. *Raymond E. Holland collection.*

A 1950s Miami candy tin. *Charliene Felts collection.* $30-35.

Palm trees line a picture frame. *Charliene Felts collection.* $10.

Flamingoes under a palm tree. A 1950s Will George flamingo. *Rasma and Bill Lowry collection.* $250.

A 1940s oil painting. *Charliene Felts collection.* $30-50.

A mangrove swamp.

An avenue of palms. *Courtesy of the Lee Island coast.*

A 1920s postcard of an avenue of palms. $1-3.

Trees at the Ringling Museum in Sarasota.

Palm tree jewelry (with sea horse pin).
Charliene Felts collection. $50.

Chapter 6
Florida Fun

Bathing beauties

Bathing beauties. *Raymond E. Holland collection.*

The sport of swimming is very much a twentieth-century phenomenon. In the nineteenth century, recreational submersion in water was called "bathing" and the clothes worn in the water were called "bathing" costumes. When Queen Victoria and her daughters "bathed" they wore an outfit of many layers called "bloomers," named after one of the leading female radicals of the day, Amelia Bloomer. By the early 1900s, women and men were both wearing more informal "bathing costumes," often made of a material called jersey, a knitted material used in the nineteenth century by the fisherman of the Isle of Jersey. Early bathing costumes for women consisted of beach shoes, a turban-style hat, and a floppy, two-piece outfit that showed little skin.

Taking the sun in the 1890s. *Raymond E. Holland collection.*

Florida beach attire in the 1880s.

By the end of the 1930s new materials and fabrics changed bathing suit design and created a new kind of leisure wear for sunbathing. Women and men wore one-piece bathing tunics that exposed the arms, but concealed the torso. In the early 1940s, DuPont invented two new materials, Nylon and Latex. In 1958, the invention of Lycra followed. With the incorporation of these new materials into swimwear, swimming soon became a sport for both men and women. The use of these fast-drying materials meant people could spend more time in the water and on the beach.

During the mid-twentieth century, society's attitudes towards swim gear also changed drastically. When the first Miss America contest was held in Atlantic City in 1921, it was more a national personality contest for pretty women. Wholesomeness rather than sex appeal swayed the judges. Even as late as the 1950s most Miss America photographs still show the winners wearing evening gowns and feminine day dresses, opposed to the bathing suits and banners worn by today's contestants.

"Kay being nautical," St. John's River, Nov. 29, 1930. *Raymond E. Holland collection.*

It wasn't just the styles of women's bathing suits that were changing. In 1933, men began to discard their tops and for the first time wore topless swimsuits. However, male modesty remained a fashion issue up to the 1960s when men stopped wearing cabana suits, the popular matching shirt and swim short outfits.

In the 1940s, Hollywood promoted bathing beauties and the sex appeal of a well-defined figure in a swimsuit. In 1944, Hollywood introduced a new bathing beauty, swim star, Esther Williams. Williams' first movie was *Bathing Beauty*.

During World War II, Hollywood pin-ups of bathing suit clad movie stars such as Betty Grable helped keep up the morale of the military. Looking back at these pin-ups, the innocence of their poses is truly amazing.

By the 1950s, bathing suit fashions were changing dramatically. Men were giving up their two-piece cabana sets and wearing briefer and briefer suits. Nudity received open acceptance on European beaches changing beach fashions forever. Women began to wear elasticized bandeaus and form-fitting elasticized bottoms. A 1957 *LIFE* magazine photograph shows women wearing "bra tops" and shorts.

In 1953, Esther Williams came to Florida and filmed *Easy to Love*. By the mid-1960s, Disney was following suit with a series of beach epics starring mouseketeer Annette Funicello. Teens flocked to the movie houses to see *Beach Party, Bikini Beach,* and *How to Stuff a Wild Bikini*.

In 1956, French director Roger Vadim and his introduction of French star and sex kitten Brigitte Bardot in the film *And God Created Woman* further challenged popular notions of beach propriety. A new age of beach wear, or lack there of, had arrived. By the 1980s, bathing suits reflected the new freedoms seen else where in American society.

Bathing beauty figurines vary in price according to age, manufacturer, and detail of figure. Early twentieth-century German and Austrian miniatures range in price from $100 and up. Japanese beauties can be bought for under $50. Most collectors prefer figures with fine facial features, and charming and intriguing poses. A rule of thumb: the more detail, the more valuable the figures are.

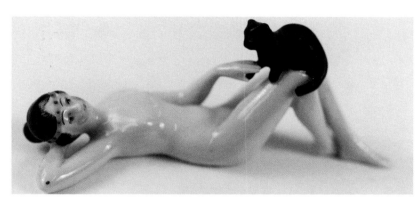

Many of the early porcelain bathing beauties were made in Austria and Germany. The figurines had a stylized beauty reminiscent of the famous flapper beauties. A 1920s German porcelain bathing beauty. *Charliene Felts collection.* $500.

A porcelain bathing beauty dressed in a bathing costume topped by a turban. Made in Occupied Japan. *Charliene Felts collection.* $75-100. (Made in Japan figures range from $40-80.)

A 1930s bathing beauty. Bathing beauties can be dated by their costumes and hairdos. *Charliene Felts collection.*

A rare 1920s German made nude mermaid on a sea horse. *Charliene Felts collection.* $200-500.

A 'naughty' bathing beauty made in Japan. "Where is the mouse." Turn her over and you will see! *Charliene Felts collection.* $75-80.

1920s-1930s Made in Japan bathing beauties. Bathing beauties can be dated by their coloring, glaze, and costume. *Charliene Felts collection.* $75-100.

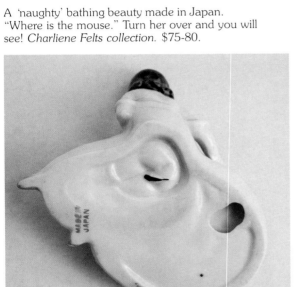

Note the elaborate turban on this bathing beauty. *Charliene Felts collection.*

This 1940s planter shows a women sporting a sailor suit and a yellow sun hat. Women didn't wear pants until the 1940s. *Charliene Felts collection.* $30-40.

1920s-1930s German bathing beauties are wearing bathing suits made from crushed shells. Crushed shell or crushed ceramic sand grain ornamentation was popular during this period. *Charliene Felts collection.* $200+.

This bathing beauty resting on a fence was made in Japan in the 1920s. *Charliene Felts collection.* $50-60.

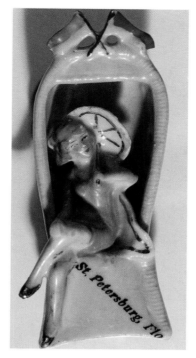

This bather sits in a typical 1930s woven beach chair. *Charliene Felts collection.*

This 1930s porcelain bathing beauty has moveable parts.

Often these souvenirs listed other destinations such as New York City. *Charliene Felts collection.* $40-60.

Even children's bathing suits were made from wool jersey. This line of children's suits sold for $1.00. *Courtesy of Sanford L. Ziff Jewish Museum of Florida.*

Bell bottom trousers were first popular in the 1940s. *Charliene Felts collection.* $75.

These "Made in Japan" bathing beauties strike different poses. *Charliene Felts collection.*

Nudity in the 1920s and 1930s was almost asexual. Note the swimmer in the background. This is an important 1920s German diver. *Charliene Felts collection.* $250.

1920s-1930s Japanese made. *Charliene Felts collection.* $80.

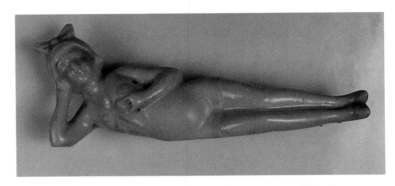

Japanese made bathing beauties frequently are depicted reclining on or near a shell. *Charliene Felts collection.* $75-100.

It's unusual to find bathing beauties in yellow costumes. Usually blue, red, and green were more popular. A 1920s-30s Japanese made figurine. *Charliene Felts collection.* $40-50.

A swimmer perched on a star. Made in Japan. *Charliene Felts collection.* $50.

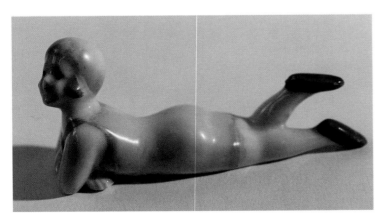

This 1920s German bathing beauty has a delightful air of innocent insouciance. *Charliene Felts collection.* $200-250.

A 1930s Japanese made swimmer admires her reflection in the pool. *Charliene Felts collection.* $85.

His and Hers salt and pepper shakers. *Charliene Felts collection.* $10-25. (Two-sided reversible figures have additional value.)

A 1930s dancer. Made in Japan. *Charliene Felts collection.*

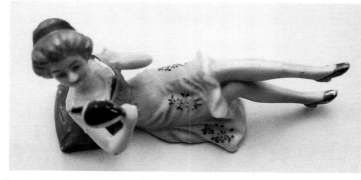

1950s souvenir plate. *Rasma and Bill Lowry collection.* $20-35.

A 1940s peek-a-boo planter. *Charliene Felts collection.*

1950s postcard showing "Water Nymphs at a Tropical Beach in Florida." $1.

A pennant with a 1950s bathing beauty on a beach of coconuts. *Rasma and Bill Lowry collection.* $3-5.

Miss Florida 1962. *Courtesy of Cypress Gardens.* $2-3.

Fishing

A Florida Marlin. *Courtesy of the Oyster House, Everglades City.*

A souvenir china fish plate. $15-20.

A blown-glass artist-made octopus on a wood burl. $75.

Souvenir salt and pepper shakers. *Rasma and Bill Lowry collection.* $10-15.

A 1960s Sears catalog advertises Japanese made pearlescent fish wall plaques. *Rasma and Bill Lowry collection.*

A postcard shows a sight-seeing pleasure boat along the Florida Intercoastal waterway. $1-2.

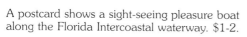

A good catch. *The George "Pete" Esthus collection.*

Catching fish Florida style. *The George "Pete" Esthus collection.*

Ted Williams catches a fish. *The George "Pete" Esthus collection.*

"Thirty-six fish each." 1930. *Raymond E. Holland collection.*

Chapter 7

Florida Fashions

Clothing & accessories

Clothes and fabrics have wide price ranges. Dresses can sell for a few dollars or, if made by a well-known designer, for up to hundreds of dollars. Vintage handbags can be bought for between $25 and $60. Fashion ties from the 1940s and 1950s sell for around $40 to $50. Good vintage clothes can cost anywhere from $25 up to hundreds of dollars depending on materials, designer if any, and where they were purchased. Obviously clothes are cheaper when found at flea markets, yard sales and thrift stores and more expensive when bought at vintage clothing stores. Used handbags can be found for $25 to $60, hats from $10 to $60, shoes for $25 and up, and dresses from $25 to $100.

Period costume jewelry varies in price from $10 to $200. Prices have a broad swing depending on where they are being sold. Good costume jewelry can range in price from $50 to $200. Collectible shops and flea markets sell enamel and souvenir pins for under $35 a piece. Sequins and rhinestones command higher prices depending on design but still can be bought for under $50. Souvenir jewelry can sell from $10 to $30. Animals bring higher prices in the $30 range.

Bakelite is another matter. Bakelite designers had a unique sense of whimsy and produced fun, funky pieces. Bakelite is really for the young at heart. Pins and bracelets start at $150 and go up and up. It is not unusual to find a Bakelite pin selling for $700, $800, or even $1000. Necklaces sell in the high hundreds. Unusual designs can sell in the $1000 dollar range. Dress clips sell around $100. The value of Bakelite is determined by color, intricacy of design, and subject matter. Red is considered among the most expensive and butterscotch, the least expensive. Pins and necklaces with dangling parts usually are more expensive. Flowers are less expensive than animals and birds. People pins such as cowboys, sailors, and clowns are highly prized and coveted by collectors.

Two fashion ties showing a definite Florida influence—flamingoes, herons, croton leaves, palm trees, coconuts, and sand. *Left:* 1950s; *right:* 1940s. $35-50.

1980s flamingo sequin-studded sunglasses. These
are the official glasses of the Flamingo 200 Club.
Rasma and Bill Lowry collection. $60-80.

1950s palm tree trimmed sunglasses.
Rasma and Bill Lowry collection. $60-80.

A Florida shirt with a palm tree design. $65-85.

1950s Florida fashion sense. *Rasma
and Bill Lowry collection.*

"Prettiest Accessories under the sun." A late 1950s
spring-summer Sears catalog showing short
cropped tops. *Rasma and Bill Lowry collection.*

1958 *Saturday Evening Post* advertisement.

Oleander is a common Florida wildflower because it is well suited to the climate, growing profusely in the presence of salt spray, and can often be seen planted in areas along the highway.

Right and below:
1950s pine needle handbags. *Rasma and Bill Lowry collection.* $45-60.

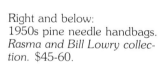

A 1940s drapery fabric. (Authentic vintage Florida patterns are valued quite high on the collectible market.) *Charliene Felts collection.* $150-225 a pair.

Shells adorn a straw handbag with a lacquered rope bottom. *Rasma and Bill Lowry collection.* $15-55.

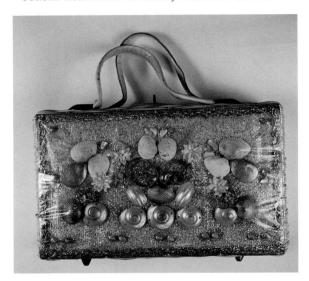

Rasma and Bill Lowry collection.

A 1950s plastic handbag showing the popular hotels and motels of the day. Motels or motor-hotels were a 1950s phenomenon. Suddenly millions of Americans were on the go and liked the idea of being able to drive up to the door and rent a room without the formality. At the same time, the idea of fast food drive-in restaurants were also becoming part of the popular scene. *Rasma and Bill Lowry collection.* $35-50.

In the 1960s, plastic, Lucite, and studded stones became popular adornments on fashion accessories. *Rasma and Bill Lowry collection.* $40-50.

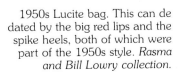

1990s tee-shirt fashions. *Andrea Nuben collection.*

1920s crocheted and coquina shells make a design statement. *Creative Collections.* $30-40.

1950s Lucite bag. This can de dated by the big red lips and the spike heels, both of which were part of the 1950s style. *Rasma and Bill Lowry collection.*

Left:
Richly-colored croton leaves predominate in a 1950s fabric. $25-35.

Right:
A photograph of a 1950s Florida wedding with palm tree decorations on the cake and palm designs on the draperies. *Charliene Felts collection.* $3-5.

A photograph of a 1950s Florida home wedding. Note the croton leaves on the draperies. *Charliene Felts collection.*

A photograph of a 1950s Florida wedding with palm trees in the background. *Charliene Felts collection.* $3-5.

A 1950s souvenir paper fan of the southern belles at Cypress Gardens. *Rasma and Bill Lowry collection.* $20-30.

1960s plastic souvenir fan. *Rasma and Bill Lowry collection.* $10-15.

1950s hand-painted fan. *Rasma and Bill Lowry collection.* $20-30.

1960s plastic souvenir fan. *Rasma and Bill Lowry collection.* $20-30.

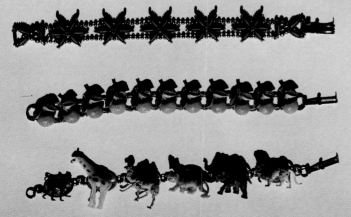

Oranges, starfish, and circus animals. Three 1950s Florida souvenir charm bracelets. *Rasma and Bill Lowry collection.* $15-25.

Florida sunshine charms. *Rasma and Bill Lowry collection.* $15-25.

1950s white plastic coral fashion jewelry. Until the 1980s white was considered a Florida color. Northern fashion ruled that white should not be worn until Memorial Day in May and could not be worn after Labor Day in September. However, in Florida, white was in fashion all year round. *Rasma and Bill Lowry collection.* $35-45.

1950s Florida souvenir charms. *Rasma and Bill Lowry collection.* $15-25.

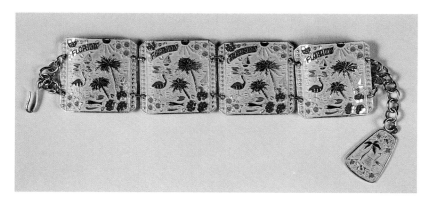

A painted aluminum charm bracelet. *Rasma and Bill Lowry collection.* $15-25.

Note the Cape Kennedy charm. Cape Canaveral was renamed Cape Kennedy after John F. Kennedy's assassination. In 1969, the name was changed back to Cape Canaveral. *Rasma and Bill Lowry collection.* $15-20.

Left:
Top: 1940s butterfly wings pin; *bottom:* 1950 transfer on glass. Butterfly wing souvenirs became very popular in the 1940s and 1950s. *Rasma and Bill Lowry collection.* $15-30. (Sterling butterfly pins made in England: $50 and up; souvenirs: $10.)

A 1980s flamingo fashion watch. *Charliene Felts collection.* $15.

1930s and 1950s Bakelite, costume rhinestones, and reverse carved Lucite pins. *Charliene Felts collection.* $25-200. Bakelite pin: $200.

1930s and 1940s costume fashion jewelry. Sterling, painted enamel, and rhinestones pins. *Charliene Felts collection.* $30-50.

Enameled and sterling pins. *Charliene Felts collection.* $75-100.

Four costume pins from the 1940s and 1950s. *Charliene Felts collection.* $20-40.

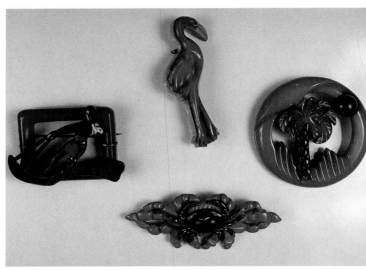

1931-1945 Bakelite crab, water skier, flamingo, and "Moon over Miami" pin with a coconut palm. Two-colored laminated Bakelite and wood and Bakelite combinations were popular stylistically. *Charliene Felts collection.* Bakelite crabs: $400 range; water skier: $300 range; "Moon over Miami:" $800-1000.

Palm trees and flamingoes. Note that the legs on one of the flamingoes is not anatomically correct. Often artists were confused by flamingo anatomy. *Charliene Felts collection.*

1940s costume jewelry. The Duchess of Windsor started the jeweled flamingo craze. This design was based on one of her pins. Flamingo fashions were inspired by the Hialeah flamingoes. *Charliene Felts collection.*

More fashion fun. Pink was a 1950s fashion color. *Charliene Felts collection.*

A Bakelite banjo-strumming frog. *Charliene Felts collection.* $3000-3500.

This is a very rare and special Bakelite flamingo bracelet and sells in the four figures. *Jack Vinales collection.* $2400.

Two fishermen, left wood and right Bakelite, and a boat to sail by. *Charliene Felts collection.* $100-400.

A late 1930s Bakelite and Lucite lobster. Lucite became popular after 1935. *Charliene Felts collection.* $250.

More Bakelite flamingoes. *Charliene Felts collection.*

Bakelite and Lucite fish. *Charliene Felts collection.*

A Bakelite bracelet, pin, and clips. *Charliene Felts collection.* $2400 range for the set.

Chapter 8
Seminole Indians

The following Seminole fashions and dolls are courtesy of Sarasota collectors *Charliene Felts, Carol Drummond, Julie Bechko,* and *Ruth-Ann Smith.*

The Seminoles were the first Floridians, and during the seventeenth and eighteenth centuries their presence was a deterrent to the expansion of white settlements. The Seminoles remained a fierce and opposing presence until the mid-nineteenth century.

Clothing

The value of Seminole clothing is determined by the number of striped patterns and the intricacy of the colors in the patterns. In the early twentieth century, the clothes were all hand sewn and made of cotton. The traditional designs used five different layers of patterning. In the 1950s, Indian craftsmen became more aware of the tourist market and started to use synthetic materials, typically cotton and poly-blend materials, and sewing machines. The result was that the stripes were reduced in number and the patterns became more stylized and less individual. Today the Indians primarily work in polyester. Collectors look for the traditional five stripes, rick rack, and intricate appliqué.

Seminole shirts, dresses, skirts, jackets, and aprons have been made for the tourist trade since the 1940s. Aprons sell for under $100. Skirts are typically $175 to $300. The prices of the skirts depend on whether or not there is appliqué and rick rack. In the 1940s, braids were hand sewn on these clothes and designs made out of hand cut and hand sewn appliqués. Rick rack is a more recent addition. Seminole fashions can sell for about $200 to $350. Older clothes with wonderful designs and handwork are worth much more.

An early twentieth-century black and white photograph. *Charliene Felts collection.*

A period postcard. *Charliene Felts collection.*

A Seminole apron.

1960s postcard.

101

1940s linen finish postcard.

102

103

Seminole dolls were made for the tourist trade out of palmetto leaves and sweet-grass. The bodies are columns made out of pressed grasses. Dolls come in two styles: those with long flowing braids and those with stiff hat-like hairdos. While these black caps look like hats, they are actually the way that the women often wore their hair for formal occasions. All dolls from the *Charliene Felts collection*.

Dolls

Seminole doll fashions reflect the costumes of the adult Indians. The Seminole dolls range in price according to size from $20 up to $150. The smaller dolls are usually under $30. Middle-sized dolls are around $60 and larger dolls can be $100 and up. Male dolls can cost between $300 and $500.

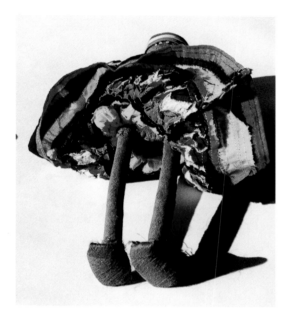

These dolls wear intricate head-dresses and beaded jewelry.

Male dolls are harder to find.
Charliene Felts collection.

A doll with a woven basket.
Charliene Felts collection. $225.

The bodies of these dolls are made from palm tree trunks and fronds. *Charliene Felts collection.*

Female dolls are more common. This is an unusual example of a male doll. *Charliene Felts collection.* $300-500.

These dolls are earlier and have no rick rack.

Early dolls' clothes were cotton. This 1970s doll is dressed in rayon. $40.

106

Chapter 9
Florida Industries

For many years Florida's tobacco farmers and cigar importers had a mutually beneficial relationship with Cuban tobacco growers. Key West and Tampa became the centers for the tobacco trade. Today, cigars remain an important industry particularly in Tampa which is the center for the cigar industry in Florida.

Collecting cigar bands was a popular hobby of the early twentieth century. Cigar manufacturers produced beautifully illustrated bands to prevent counterfeiters from passing off inferior brands of cigars. Most collectors select bands and labels with ornate designs, famous people, animals, beautiful women, cars, and/or historical events.

Cigar collectibles have never caught on as popular collectibles. Plates sell for $35 to $85. Books and albums of cigar labels sell for under $100. Individual bands and labels have limited value.

Cigars

A 1930s plate decorated with cigar labels and bands. *Creative Collections.* $45 and up depending on size.

Left:
A 1950s glossy postcard. *Rasma and Bill Lowry collection.*

Another version of a cigar souvenir plate. *Creative collections.*

Cigar bands. *Creative Collections*. Individual pages vary in price according to subject. A Shirley Temple cigar band page with 8 to a page sells for $75.

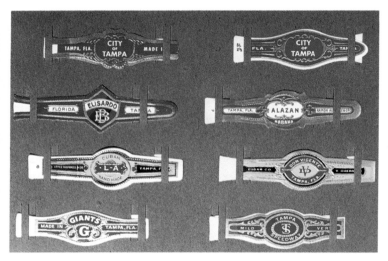

Collecting cigar bands was a popular hobby in the early twentieth century. Cigar bands were covered with ornate designs and images of famous people, animals, beautiful women, cars, and historical events. This is a cover of a cigar band album. *Creative Collections*. Albums: $95.

Making a souvenir plate was a popular hobby. *Creative Collections.*

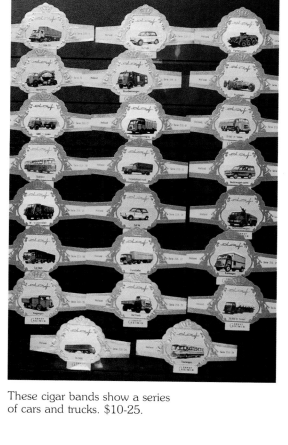

These cigar bands show a series of cars and trucks. $10-25.

Making cigar bands and labels was big business. This is a dye stamp. *Eryc Atwood collection.* $45-60.

These bands show the variety of images used.

These show more of the variety of these illustrations.

Oranges & the Citrus Industry

Initially, Florida was an agricultural economy based first on cattle, then cotton, and later oranges, limes, and grapefruit. The area around Orlando was at one time a cattle center exporting cattle to Cuba, and cotton to the rest of the United States. However, the devastating hurricane of 1871 destroyed most of the cotton fields, forcing Florida farmers to look for another crop.

Ponce de Leon and his men are credited with planting the first orange seeds. However, the citrus industry's roots began with the Franciscan missionaries who first grew oranges and lemons as early as the 1600s. The first grapefruit tree was planted by a Frenchman in 1806. In 1823, he also planted the first grapefruit grove near Tampa. By the late 1880s, more of the swamplands were drained and developed, and, by the late 1890s, the citrus industry had begun to grow in earnest with the introduction of a hardier strain of orange and grapefruit.

Orange collectibles are still regarded as kitsch and as such their prices depend on the visual appeal of the items. Prices range from $5 to $40. Labels are priced at $2 to $5 unless they are of particular historic value. Labels must be in good condition and not torn.

A colorful 1955 Florida engagement calendar showing orange groves. *Rasma and Bill Lowry collection.* $10-25.

1890s Florida scenes. *Raymond E. Holland collection.*

A glossy souvenir orange postcard from the 1960s. *Rasma and Bill Lowry collection.* $1-3.

1940s linen postcard. $2-3.

This 1960s souvenir handkerchief can be dated by the name Cape Kennedy and the two-piece bathing suit with a modified bikini bottom. *The George "Pete" Esthus collection.* $10-15.

An Atwood grapefruit label. *The George "Pete" Esthus collection.* $2-5.

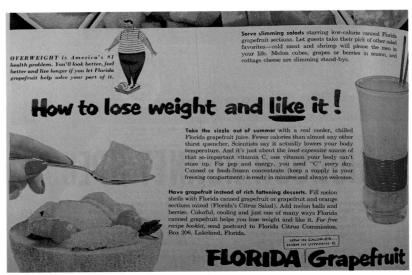

"How to Lose weight and like it!" A Florida grapefruit ad. May 22, 1954. *Saturday Evening Post advertisement. Rasma and Bill Lowry collection.*

A vintage turpentine maul used by farm workers. *Eryc Atwood collection.* $50-60.

"It's always time for Florida Orange Juice." *Rasma and Bill Lowry collection.*

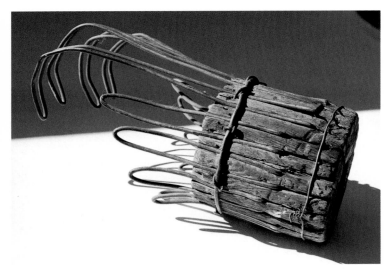

An orange picking instrument. *Eryc Atwood collection.* $30-40.

A 1930s fruit cake tin with a nice lithograph design. $15-20.

Orange people. Two sets of 1950s ceramic and plastic salt and pepper shakers. *Rasma and Bill Lowry collection.* $15-25.

Everyone comes home with coconut patty candies from Florida.

1950s beaded and sequined oranges. This was a popular craft project of the 1950s and 1960s. *Rasma and Bill Lowry collection.* $15-25.

A ceramic orange dish from the 1960s. $10-15.

Orange maracas. *Rasma and Bill Lowry collection.* $15-25.

1950s "orange people:" salt and peppers and a measuring spoon holder. *Rasma and Bill Lowry collection.* $10-15.

The Tropicana orange juice company, which is based in Bradenton, has had many popular give-away premiums. This Tropicana transistor orange radio was a popular one in the 1960s. This set of orange pig salt and pepper shakers was also a popular 1950-1960 souvenir. *Rasma and Bill Lowry collection.* $15-40.

1960s toothpick holder and cream and sugar set. *Rasma and Bill Lowry collection.* $15-30.

An orange chalkware string puller, made in Japan, was a popular souvenir item in the 1940s and 1950s. String pullers have become popular collectibles. $20-25.

1950s redware "Tomato people" salt and pepper shakers. *Rasma and Bill Lowry collection.* $85.

1940s chalkware wall plaque. *Rasma and Bill Lowry collection.* $25-35.

A Florida lime.

A 1960s acrylic lime trivet with real lime pits imbedded inside. *Creative Collections.* $30-35.

1950s Florida taffy box. Note the two-piece bathing suits. $10-15.

Ever since the late 1890s, the desire for a pleasant year-round climate has brought millions of tourists to Florida each year. Today tourism has become one of Florida's biggest industries.

A 1950s Weeki Wachee Spring luggage label. $5-10.

1950s Florida luggage label. $5-10.

A 1950s luggage label. In 1924, the only way one could cross Tampa Bay was by way of the Bee Line Ferry, which cost $1.75 a car. In 1954, the first Tampa Bay bridge was built. It was named the Sunshine Skyway to the Sea. In 1987, it was replaced by the present more streamlined bridge. *Rasma and Bill Lowry collection.* $10.

Chapter 10

Entertainment

The Ringling Brothers & Barnum & Bailey Circus

Ernest Hemingway called the circus "the only ageless delight you can buy for money." And, since the early 1920s, Sarasota has been known as Florida's circus city. The Ringlings first discovered Sarasota in the 1900s. By 1927, they had set up their winter headquarters in a field on the outskirts of the city.

The Ringling Brothers and Barnum and Bailey Circus owes its start to one man, Phineas T. Barnum, who made his first fortune as a circus entrepreneur in 1835 when he hired Joice Heth, supposed to be 161 years old and the former nurse of George Washington. Barnum exhibited Joice in New York and New England and made more than $1500 a week. His next coup was to buy the Scudder's American Museum in New York and lure people into paying two admission fees by posting a misleading sign "This way to the Egress." Egress, of course, meant exit and once outside there was only one way to get back in and that was to buy another ticket.

By 1870, the Barnum Grand Circus was the largest circus in America and was traveling nationwide. In 1872, Barnum declared it "the greatest show on earth." By 1881, he had joined forces with James Bailey who would eventually sell part of the Barnum and Bailey Circus to the five Ringling Brothers of Wisconsin.

As a side note, the *New York Sun* [newspaper] agreed to run Barnum's obituary while he was still alive so he could read it. At Bailey's death, the Ringling Brothers bought out Bailey's controlling shares. Today, the Ringling Brothers and Barnum and Bailey Circus still upholds its title as "the Greatest Show on Earth."

Unless otherwise noted, all circus memorabilia is from the *George "Pete" Esthus collection.*

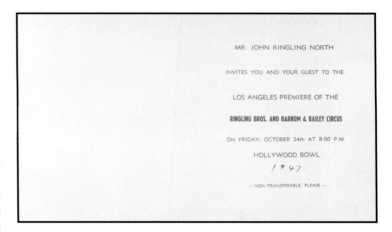

MR. JOHN RINGLING NORTH
INVITES YOU AND YOUR GUEST TO THE
LOS ANGELES PREMIERE OF THE
RINGLING BROS. AND BARNUM & BAILEY CIRCUS
ON FRIDAY, OCTOBER 24th AT 8:00 P.M.
HOLLYWOOD BOWL
1947
— NON-TRANSFERABLE, PLEASE —

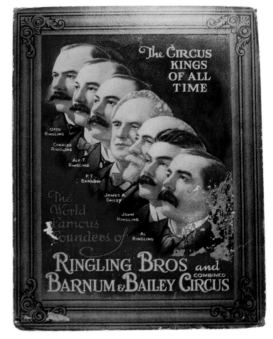

"Lotus" says —
"Thanks again for everything — Much appreciated"

Ringling Bros. and Barnum & Bailey
Combined Shows, Inc.

These mirthful, merrymaking madcaps, the clowns, are a regular part of the circus acts at THE CIRCUS HALL OF FAME in Sarasota, Florida. Popular pranksters, "Bob-O", "Victor", and "Coco" have appeared at the U.S. 41 attraction.

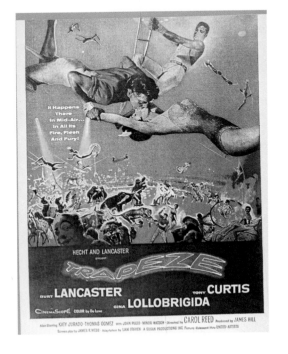

To My Good Buddy PETE, The man with Keys to success. On With the Show! Ringmasterly yours,

AMERICA'S MOST CELEBRATED RINGMASTER

RINGLING BROS AND BARNUM & BAILEY COMBINED SHOWS INC

10 ROCKEFELLER PLAZA   NEW YORK

VIA AIR MAIL

AIR MAIL
5¢
UNITED STATES OF AMERICA

Mr. Leif Osmundsen
Ringling Bros. and Barnum
& Bailey, Comb. Shows, Inc.
P. O. Box 789,
Sarasota, Florida

FOR LEIF OSMUNDSEN

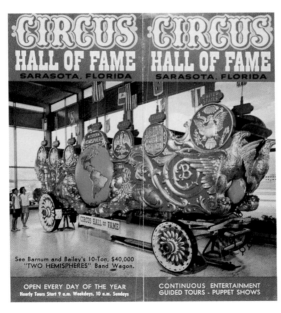

CIRCUS CIRCUS
HALL OF FAME   HALL OF FAME
SARASOTA, FLORIDA   SARASOTA, FLORIDA

CIRCUS HALL OF FAME

See Barnum and Bailey's 10-Ton, $40,000
"TWO HEMISPHERES" Band Wagon.

OPEN EVERY DAY OF THE YEAR
Hourly Tours Start 9 a.m. Weekdays, 10 a.m. Sundays

CONTINUOUS ENTERTAINMENT
GUIDED TOURS - PUPPET SHOWS

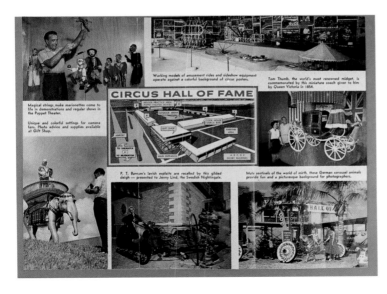

Working models of amusement rides and sideshow equipment operate against a colorful background of circus posters.

Tom Thumb, the world's most renowned midget, is commemorated by this miniature coach given to him by Queen Victoria in 1854.

Magical strings make marionettes come to life in demonstrations and regular shows in the Puppet Theater.

Unique and colorful settings for camera fans. Photo advice and supplies available at Gift Shop.

CIRCUS HALL OF FAME

P. T. Barnum's lavish exploits are recalled by this gilded sleigh — presented to Jenny Lind, the Swedish Nightingale.

Mute sentinels of the world of mirth, these German carousel animals provide fun and a picturesque background for photographers.

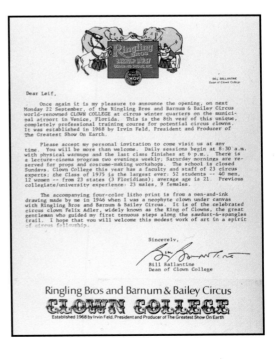

BILL BALLANTINE
Dean of Clown College

Dear Leif,

Once again it is my pleasure to announce the opening, on next Monday 22 September, of the Ringling Bros and Barnum & Bailey Circus world-renowned CLOWN COLLEGE at circus winter quarters on the municipal airport in Venice, Florida. This is the 8th year of this unique, completely professional training course for potential circus clowns. It was established in 1968 by Irvin Feld, President and Producer of The Greatest Show On Earth.

Please accept my personal invitation to come visit us at any time. You will be more than welcome. Daily sessions begin at 8:30 a.m. with physical warmups and the last class finishes at 6 p.m. There is a lecture-cinema program two evenings weekly; Saturday mornings are reserved for props and costume-making workshops. The school is closed Sundays. Clown College this year has a faculty and staff of 23 circus experts; the Class of 1975 is the largest ever: 52 students -- 40 men, 12 women -- from 23 states (3 Floridians); average age is 21. Previous collegiate/university experience: 23 males, 9 females.

The accompanying four-color litho print is from a pen-and-ink drawing made by me in 1946 when I was a neophyte clown under canvas with Ringling Bros and Barnum & Bailey Circus. It is of the celebrated circus clown Felix Adler, widely known as the King of Clowns, the great gentleman who guided my first tenuous steps along the sawdust-&-spangles trail. I hope that you will welcome this modest work of art in a spirit of circus fellowship.

Sincerely,

Bill Ballantine
Dean of Clown College

Ringling Bros and Barnum & Bailey Circus
CLOWN COLLEGE
Established 1968 by Irvin Feld, President and Producer of The Greatest Show On Earth

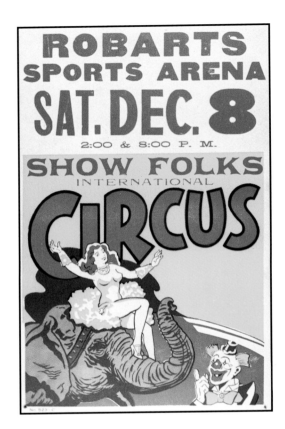

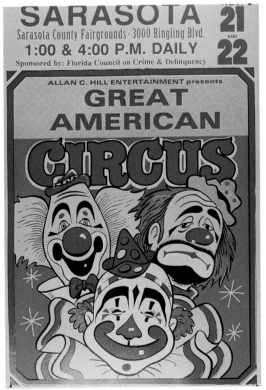

This is a view from Ca' Z'an, the Ringlings' Venetian palazzo. All the patio doors are hand-blown stained glass.

The Ringling coat of arms.

A 1956 record album of circus music.
Rasma and Bill Lowry collection. $10.

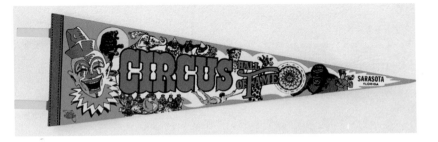

Movies

Capitalizing on the popularity of the circus, Cecil de Mille filmed *The Greatest Show on Earth* in Sarasota in 1951, which used many of the Ringling stars and attractions. It went on to become one of Florida's most famous films. De Mille's stars—Charleton Heston, Betty Grable, Cornel Wilde, Dorothy Lamour, and Gloria Grahame—worked along side native Sarasotans who were hired at $.75 as extras to fill the "Big Top."

In 1953, another movie star favorite, Esther Williams, came to Sarasota to film *Easy to Love*. In order to replicate the underwater dancing made famous by the Weeki Wachee mermaids, the studio built her a customized pool just for the film.

Sports

The all-American sport of baseball came to Florida as early as the 1920s when the New York Giants made Sarasota their spring practice home. In 1933, the Boston Red Sox made Payne Park their spring training headquarters and Ted Williams was one of the many famous players who practiced there. In 1960, the Red Sox left and the White Sox moved in and took their place. Today, Florida is a paradise for all athletes, both professional and amateur.

Bobby Riggs was one of many famous tennis stars who came to Florida. $5.

Peter Lawford (above) was Esther Williams' co-star in "Easy to Love" and made quite a splash himself when he visited Sarasota. *The George "Pete" Esthus collection.* $5.

ALAN STEPHAN, "Mr. America" 1946, has developed one of the worlds most amazing physiques through the intelligent use of Barbells. His body is a perfect example of Herculean proportions and physical power that goes with it.

Babe Zacharias plays golf. $3-5.

MEMBER — ADVISORY STAFF *Wilson* SPORTING GOODS CO.

MEMBER — ADVISORY STAFF *Wilson* SPORTING GOODS CO.

Single pennants can
cost from $5 and up.

1941 vintage pennants. *Eryc Atwood collection.* $25.

Playing cards

Playing card collectors judge a package of cards by the box cover. We have tried to include cards that are commercial, historic, and just too pretty to pass up. The origin of card games goes back to ancient times when players used bits of bones, dominoes, tokens, money, coins, and shells to lay wagers. Card games were most popular in Victorian times when families began to enjoy home leisure time. Social games like bridge, canasta, poker, and gin rummy are among the most popular card games today.

Playing cards are most valuable when they come in a complete set, are in almost mint condition, have colorful images and/or packaging, well-known logos, or interesting illustrations. Generally, they sell in the $5 to $50 range. Most card sets are priced from $5 to $10. Earlier sets can be valued at $25 and up. Playing cards are a particularly nice collectible because they take up little space and are functional. Some of the cards pictured here show the seal of Florida, the logos of Flagler's trains, and typical Florida scenes.

Playing card decks come in two categories, souvenir and historical. The historical cards showing old trains, old Florida places, and/or places of historical interest can cost $85 to $100. Generic souvenir decks cost $5.

The Bok Singing Tower in Lake Wales is a popular tourist attraction.

These are earlier cards. $50-100.

Salt & pepper shakers

Salt and pepper shakers vary in price from $10 to $25 unless they have particular historic interest or an unusual subject matter.

A 1960s hand-painted ceramic set. *Charliene Felts collection.* $10.

1950s hand-painted plastic. *Charliene Felts collection.* $10-20.

Salt and pepper snowdomes. *Rasma and Bill Lowry collection.* $25-35.

A set of ceramic flamingoes in opposing views. *Charliene Felts collection.* $20-25.

Late 1930s hand-painted glass salt and pepper shakers with a Bakelite look on the tops. *Charliene Felts collection.* $50.

A back view.

127

Two souvenir salt and pepper shakers from Sunken Gardens in opposing views. It was very popular to portray a set of flamingoes in opposing positions. *Charliene Felts collection.* $10.

1950s hand-painted plastic set. Pink and black are typical 1950s colors. *Charliene Felts collection.* $25.

Charliene Felts collection. $20-30.

Souvenir China

Souvenir china generally is priced from $5 to $60. Pricing is determined by size, date, condition, and imagery. Small plates fall in the range of $10 to $15. Medium-sized plates value $20 to $35 and larger plates can bring in anything from a few dollars up to $90. If a plate is signed, it is worth more. If it was manufactured by a known factory or in Occupied Japan, it is obviously worth more. Hand painted plates have more value than decal transfers. Many of the 1940s and 1950s plates were sold in dime stores, the equivalent of today's souvenir shops. Gold-trimmed plates were typical of the 1950s.

Ashtrays can cost $10 to $75 depending on age, design, material, and historic value, i.e., a famous hotel ashtray would be worth around $50 and up. Vintage porcelain or painted metal ashtrays have more value than glass or plastic ones. Funky plastic always has an intrinsic value of its own.

Silver Springs English Staffordshire sold by Ray Davidson in Silver Springs. The back of the plate reads: "Nature's Underwater Fairyland. The largest flowing springs in the world . . . over 750 million gallons daily . . . greatest depth is 80 feet." $50-75.

This is a decal transfer plate.

This tray was given out as a souvenir give-a-away by Badcock Home Furnishings, a popular Florida home furnishings chain. $15-20.

Postcards

People have always written home and postcards evolved as a convenient, shorter form of communication. Today we can date postcards by the color, design, and texture of the printing. The styles of the hairdos, bathing suits, and automobiles, for example, shown on the front of postcards can also help date them. Early postcards have a dappled, faded look. Later cards adopted a kind of surreal technicolor. Today's postcards are airbrushed and show a higher quality of printing technique.

In the late 1890s and early 1900s, people sent private mailing cards. Postcards of the early 1900s had undivided backs. Beginning around 1907 and continuing through 1920, postcards had divided backs, with a separation between the area for the address and message. Around 1915 through 1930 postcards began to have a white border around the front image. Linen finish postcards were first produced in the 1930s and continued to be manufactured through the mid 1940s. Polychromed colored postcards were popular in the 1950s and glossy postcards were first circulated in the 1960s.

Moonlights and flowers have been popular subjects for Florida postcards since the turn of the century. Early tourist cards showed beaches. Later flamingoes and garden spots became popular.

Postcard prices begin at $.25 and can go up to $5. Historical postcards begin at $15 and up. Naughty postcards are priced at $1 and up.

An 1880s postcard of an early steamship. "We never missed a meal" bragged the writer. In the 1800s and early 1900s, waters were often so rough that sea sickness was an inevitable part of the travel experience. $3-5.

This is an early tourist card showing the "illuminated Ocklawaha Forest." $1-3.

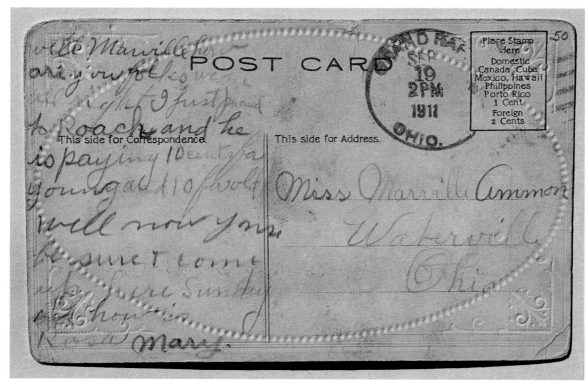

A 1911 postcard. Note the divided back. If the card wasn't dated, the divided back would tell you it was from 1907-1915. $3-5.

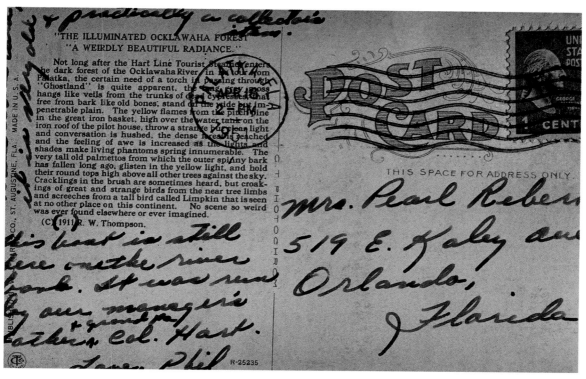

THIS SPACE FOR ADDRESS ONLY.

Although this card was mailed in 1951, it is a vintage card. The message reads "This postcard is very old and practically a collector's item." $1-3.

Finest Beach in the World.

Daytona Beach in the 1900s.

Daytona in the 1920s.

This is one of the many linen-textured postcards from the years 1930-1945. In those days, "palm beaches" referred to Florida beaches. Today the name is associated with the Greater Palm Beach area. *Raymond E. Holland collection.* $2-5.

1930s "Moon over Miami" was a popular image of the 1930s-1940s. $2-5.

A very unusual 1920s orange-shaped postcard.
Rasma and Bill Lowry collection. $10-15.

A 1940s postcard from St. Petersburg
made out of cypress wood. $10.

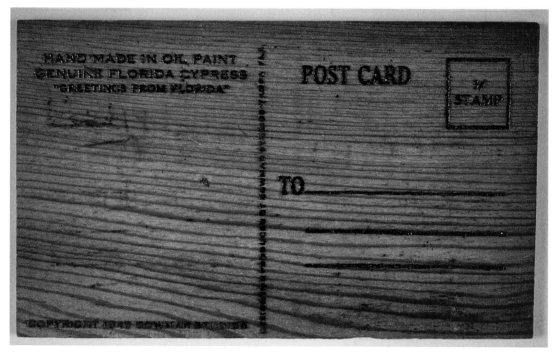

The cover of a 1939 postcard set from the Gulf Coast. $5.

Merchants used postcards as a form of free advertising.

The Gulf Coast had to try harder. 1940s.

Moonlights have been popular with tourists since the 1900s.

Sunrise on the Halifax River.

BATHING BY MOONLIGHT, FLORIDA

This is an early postcard from 1917 showing a Florida moonlight.
Note the hat silhouettes in the moonlight. $5-10.

DH-34—Moonlight over Hollywood Beach, Fla.

1940s-1950s. $5-10.

Moonlight on Biscayne Bay, Coconut Grove, Miami, Florida

Sailing at Sunset upon a Peaceful Lake in Florida 190

This is a good example of a polychrome-colored postcard. These glossy colors were used beginning in 1939 and created images that were often more surreal-looking than real. $5-8.

D.C. 14 Moon at Miami Beach, Fla.

142

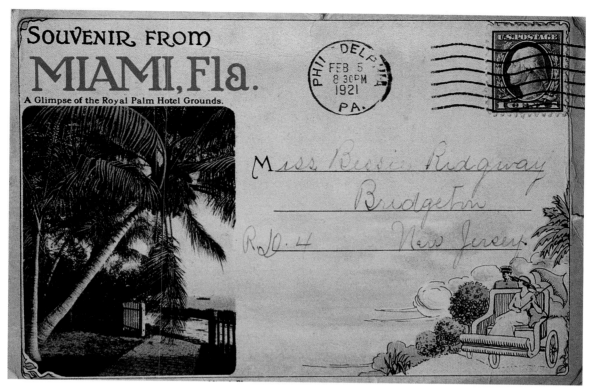

A postcard of 1921 Miami showing a glimpse of Flagler's Royal Palm Hotel. $4-7.

"Moon over Miami," 1930s. $3.

EVERY DAY SCENE AT MIAMI BEACH.

Every day scene at Miami Beach. $1.

The author's father sent her this card in 1952. It was his first trip to Florida. He took the train, spent a week in the sun at the Fontainebleau Hotel, fished, and went to the races at Hialeah. The next year he drove his family down for a two week winter vacation and stayed at the more informal Indian Creek Hotel.

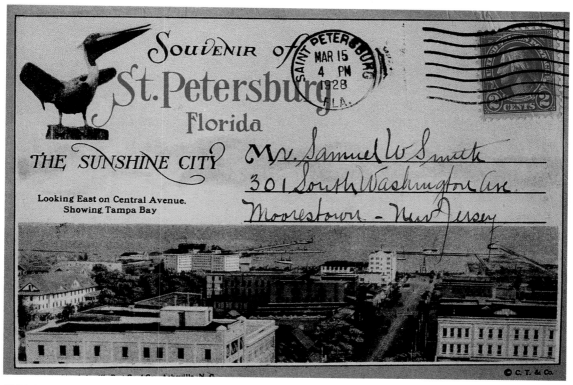

1928 St. Petersburg.

1928 Sanford, Florida, on the St. John's River.

TEMPERATURE
JUST RIGHT
IN BEAUTIFUL
FLORIDA

In the 1940s and 1950, cartoonish, double entendre girlie cards and 'north and south' postcards also became popular. $12-15. (Politically incorrect statements or illustrations add value.)

ENJOYING THE FLORIDA SUNSHINE

Two vintage 1950s postcards. $1-3.

Two "gloating" postcards. $1-3.

147

Two more.

Blossoms

Sunshine Skyway Bridge

Sunshine Skyway Bridge

The two bridges, 1954 and 1987. This is an unusual postcard and highly collectible because there were few remaining views of both bridges existing side by side. Notice there is still visible traces of the damage from the 1980 crash with the freighter. $10.

Florida's Sunshine Skyway

Since the 1980s, South Beach has experienced a successful renaissance and the old Art Deco hotels from the 1940s and 1950s have never looked as good. A postcard of the South Beach Century Hotel in its heyday in the 1940s and 1950s. $1-3.

Snowdomes

One of the most popular souvenirs is the snowdome. Creating "good" snow has challenged inventors for years. Originally the "snow" was pieces of shattered pottery. Snowdomes can be dated by the quality of their "snow fall." Early domes were made out of glass. Plastic became more common in the 1960s and 1970s. Today many snowdomes use glitter rather than the traditional snow.

Snowdomes are priced from $5 to $20. Their value is determined by their age, subject matter, quality of "snow," and historical significance. Glass domes are more valuable than the newer, plastic ones. Collectors are always on the lookout for better quality images and "snow."

Left: traditional "snow" when shaken; *right:* present day snow domes no longer have "snow." Instead, they have glitter.

This is an older glass dome. $45 and up.

In the 1970s, more and more snowdomes began to have moveable parts. Note the see-saw. $15-18. (Figures add more value.)

This is another snowdome with moveable parts.

This snowdome was a home craft model. Note all the special trim pasted to the rim. $10.

Calendars

A 1900s perpetual calendar. *Raymond E. Holland collection.* $10-15.

A mechanical calendar. $10.

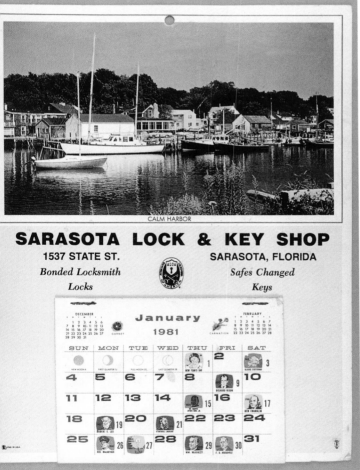

CALM HARBOR

AUTUMN DISPLAY

Yardsticks

Throughout the world, businessman recognize the value of advertising and marketing their products. With many Americans doing their own home repairs and working with their hands, the yardstick is not only a useful and necessary tool, but can be a colorful means of advertisement and a souvenir with practical uses.

Price wise, yardsticks are an uncharted field. We suspect that while they are fun to collect, the price range is only about $1 to $2.

All yardsticks are from *The George "Pete" Esthus collection.*

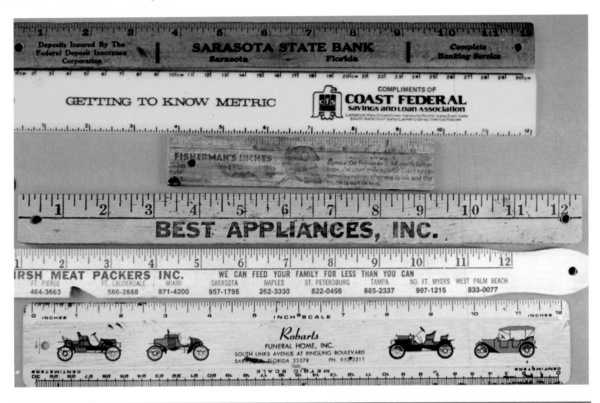

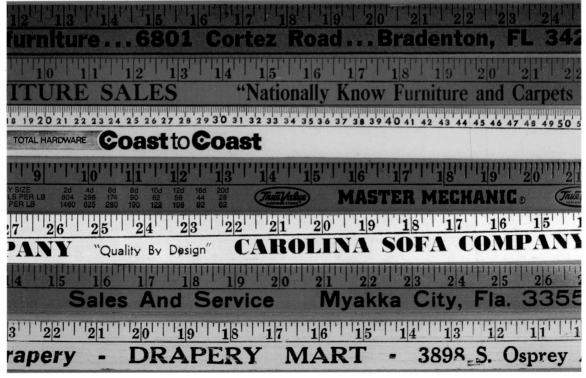

STANDARD AUTO PARTS CO.   1517

THE BARNICHOL - THE BEST LITTLE H.

Sarasota - St. Pete. - Orlando - Gainesville -

3   1066 CENTRAL AVE., SARASOTA, FLA.

1960 21st Street, Sarasota — *Fuel Oil* — **Pho**

At the end of the day nothing is more relaxing than a walk on the beach or watching another beautiful Florida sunset.

Resources

Addresses

Creative Collections
527 South Pineapple Avenue
Sarasota, Florida 34236
(941) 951-0477

Sarasota Jungle Gardens
3701 Bayshore Road
Sarasota, Florida 34234
(941) 355-5305

Sarasota Lock and Key Shop
The Esthus Collection
1537 State Street
Sarasota, Florida 34236
(941) 953-3773

Visit Florida
661 East Jefferson, Suite 300
Tallahassee, Florida 32301
(850) 488-5607

Lee Island Coast Visitor and Convention Bureau
2180 West First Street, Suite 200
Fort Myers, Florida 33901
1-800-237-6441

Orlando/Orange County Convention & Visitors Bureau
6700 Forum Drive, Suite 100
Orlando, Florida 32821-8017

Flagler Museum
One Whitehall Way
Palm Beach, Florida 33480
(561) 655-2833

St. Augustine Alligator Farm
Route A1A South
P.O. 9005
St. Augustine, Florida 32085
(904) 824-3337

Cypress Gardens
P.O. Box 1
Cypress Gardens, Florida 33884
1-800-282-2123
(941) 324-2111

Daytona Beach Area Convention and Visitors Bureau
126 East Orange Avenue
Daytona Beach, Florida 32114
(904) 255-0415 or 1-800-544-04150

Miami-Dade County
Historical Preservation Division
140 West Flagler Street, Suite 1102
Miami, Florida 33130-1561
(305) 375-3471

South Beach Marketing Council
(305) 538-0090

Miami Design Preservation League
(305) 672-2014

Sanford L. Ziff Jewish Museum of Florida
301 Washington Avenue
Miami Beach, Florida 33139-6965
(305) 672-5044